Rob Halpern

[———]

PLACEHOLDER

ENITHARMON PRESS

First published in 2015
by Enitharmon Press
10 Bury Place
London WC1A 2JL

www.enitharmon.co.uk

Distributed in the UK by
Central Books
99 Wallis Road
London E9 5LN

Distributed in the USA and Canada by
Independent Publishers Group
814 North Franklin Street
Chicago, IL 60610
USA
www.ipgbook.com

ISBN: 978-1-907587-89-4

Enitharmon Press gratefully acknowledges the financial support of
Arts Council England, through Grants for the Arts.

British Library Cataloguing-in-Publication Data.
A catalogue record for this book is available
from the British Library.

Cover: Untitled collage, by Tanya Hollis and Rob Halpern (2011)

Selections from *Common Place* are published in tandem with
Ugly Duckling Presse, Brooklyn NY

Selections from *Music for Porn* are reprinted with the permission of
The Permissions Company, Inc., on behalf of
Nightboat Books, www.nightboat.org

Designed in Albertina by Libanus Press
and printed in England by SRP

for my mom & dad

CONTENTS

MUSIC FOR PORN

DISASTER SUITE

COMMON PLACE

WEAK LINKS

There are so many things I want to tell you, things that embarrass me most, though it's hard to voice any one of them, even for you, whom I've come to trust. So far, all my writing amounts to these strategies of evasion. That's what I was telling Dana & Lee, sitting outside in the late August heat, as we tried to grasp where it all might be going. Casting idols on my brain, the sun produces these false appearances, the dahlias burning under gunmetal skies, so I've yet to discover what real life feels like. At least that's what I tell them. But what I want to tell you is, well, take my body, for example, a place where incommensurables collide *rhetoric & blood, price & value, datum & event* the bad equivalent of a hole in a soldier's bladder before he's given the form to join the donor's club. The dialectic, having come to such dumb arrest, yields this taxonomy of wounds pasted to a straw man I'll never fuck, a cheap shot at militarization, its so-called human face. What figure do combatants cut against a company that earns the bulk of its twelve billion in annual revenue from army contracts, and whose product tracks my car as it moves thru any one of eight hundred Oakland intersections. This is why my book amounts to a simple X without the algebra to resolve its value in a world where the word 'decorative' modifies unintelligible things, thereby assisting sales. As in every cash-starved city, the promise of federal dollars makes military surveillance an easy cow. See what I mean, in the absence of incident, structure eludes, the poem being but the gesture of a body groping its own withdrawn architecture. Whether bound or bundled, all my usable parts compress to the volume of a prosthetic device shoved inside a foreign orifice. This is how capital explodes in song, usurping the air you might be privately singing, the way the very idea of the flood dries up after the deluge. That's so dutifully Rimbaud, but what would the equivalent be? After the idea of collapse recedes, my use of disjunction will bear no relation to a break in the chain of title, a detainee's autopsy report, or any old forensic audit robo-signed & withdrawn in hazy spells of law. But nothing appears to accumulate inside the hole my organ makes when, mortally wounded in a grenade attack, his blown genitals get contracted to a public utility, a city square or park, this being but an asset to securitize, a convention by whose rhyme scheme 'scars' and 'cars' seem to be of common scale, a sound to sing no polis. Who can accommodate such rules when the totality penetrates yr colon, absorbs yr shit, the very thing that arouses my pleasure and can't be absorbed by narration, soothed by his big dead muscle. With the help of newly calibrated nite-vision goggles, we'll eventually retrieve what bodies will have been interred from yet another abandoned future [————] here among the low-slung concrete municipal buildings, location of my operative and verse. If the incompletion theorem is correct and any account of a logically coherent system must contain at least one radical instance that can't be contained by that account, then my soldier's wound must be just such an instance, a hole in sense, our common place, nonsite of suffering under current conditions, negative imprint of all my social relations, resistant to story though submissive to an allegory turned against the conceptual purity of its own redemptive function, bearing no resemblance to my form. Having mistaken securitization for security, whatever it is my body craves has already been sold as the normal way of belonging to the things that own me. With the sap that keeps me in bed with my financialized double, I adhere to the aggregate of productive labor hours necessary to repay what I owe, which daily exceeds my waking life. Ever since my last anonymous fuck, I've been feeling totally adrift in dark liquidity pools, thinking about Greece and Portugal, or my dad's diminishing bank account, though I can barely keep all this in my head, currency flux being the means to ensure my hope in retirement, the hedge around my bed being taller than I can scale, so many new instruments & futures, asset values expanding at 3% per annum as all my so-called friendships become sites of monetary extraction. With the outsourcing of such suffering, the meaning of my rhyme depreciates to the size of a soldier's impotent nut, upon which I've fallen in hard times. I mean, when it's the leg that gets enjambed by precision rather than a line of verse, these are the extremes to which one's gotta go to overcome the mind/body split, the truth of abjection being an effect of objective falsehood. So my poems patrol the perimeter of popular speech, the bodies I sing of, being militarized form, each sentence an enclosure, like the globe itself, this emblem of sovereignty, where our relations exist inside systems of yield and harvest, as organ and seed enhance the dearness of my product. Dying from this illusion of scarcity, each abstract universal fails the concrete assertion of material life, or remains excluded from it like his "esophagus lined by gray-white mucous". Who can out-perform the rules when the financial unconscious becomes a poltergeist, my house organizing appetite and shit in equal measure with my poem. Dead music on the floor, the time of life being anti-matter, a body pocked w/ decimals, distilled in a column of digits gracing page D6 where I've found love in bio-ruin while my body burns in each commutable decision to buy or sell. And as if to pass the time, or trick the labor that makes time real, I've taken to transcribing autopsy reports by hand, as if a conceptual procedure *any act of writing* could bring the bodies closer, or at least denote the wounds. This is how my soldier becomes a Gitmo detainee. I was cruising for army guys, but each visible scar is a portal to the same invisible disease, interminable deten-tion and enteral feeding. I mean, how long can a body go on testing the load bearing capacity of militarized social networks wherein what needs to be negated are the condi-tions that enable anyone to declare "the subject is dead", by which I mean the Yemeni man whose name's been redacted [(b)(6)] at the top of this report, a civilian non-combatant found unresponsive with a ligature around his neck in a cell at the Behavior Health Unit, Joint Task Force Guantanamo Bay, Cuba, at approximately 2200 hours on an elided date in 2009. But the so-called "subject" might just as easily point to a place in my poem, a form the body assumes in language though in excess of any grammatical position, like the one that binds my double to the private who'd replace him. Falling prey to nonsense, my writing denotes nothing but the apparatus that makes the corpus mean, a common grave, a ditch or sink, where ID fails and leaves the bodies nameless. I can't stop wondering what it would feel like to arouse relation at the place of its derealization inside his "gastric mucosa, arranged in the usual rugal folds and unremarkable", or beside "the underlying renal cortices, sharply delineated from the medullary pyramids, which are purple to tan and unremarkable." My bladder floats in the same somatic void from which his meat's been drawn, quartered and sublimed into medium where love destroys its object, failing to distinguish opposites, the pleural cavity itself depriving the body of any singularity in excess of the process that has tagged its parts. I don't mean severe facial trauma and right leg amputation, nor lower-left leg fracture and pulmonary embolism, nor left leg prosthesis and shrapnel lesion, but the reported appearance of his "unremarkable genitalia", extraordinarily rendered. Which gets me thinking about my first fuck, a boy named Andy, to whose personal ad I desperately responded in the Amherst Valley Voice with a hand-written letter in 1984 after years of interminable fantasy failed to materialize the flesh I craved, and whose genitals were anything but unremarkable. Note how my reference to handwriting forges a link between the autopsy report and my memory of doing it with Andy in the woods on my dad's camp blanket, which may have been army-issued back in the forties, and which I'd grown accustomed to keeping in the car just in case, though I can't tell you what I was thinking, I mean, it was dark, and the trees at the foot of that modest peak on the edge of town were thick, but the link between a detainee's organ function and my lousy arousal was already there, haunting psychic backwash, just waiting to be triggered. This is all very fresh, but I can't remember when I first imagined my body being pummeled by a soldier's dirty slab, the feeding tube being of more recent provenance, like the formless drape over the abyss his legs create, or an abscess in meat processed at the US base just outside Kabul. Food, being the materialization of this estrangement, the thing about the old days, well, 'they the old days', and while new rules allow photographs of casualties, the prohibition on recognizable faces and other identifiable features persists, ostensibly to protect the family. What I finally want to confess is that I've failed the promise of the poem, the hoary "house of being" being another name for market stress, or house arrest, or whatever binds me to the particulate matter of causal force, bone-dust. As Blake would have it, the elect can't be redeemed from heaps of smoking rubble, a blank in nature money rushes in to fill, but I'm still trying to sense the feeling of this form. I've even learned to respond to the need by heart and feel myself reaching for a friend, these scenes of recent enclosure, my detainee's body being the hazardous substrate of all the stuff we don't produce but upon which the dream of our wellbeing hangs, a gift from nowhere, like darkness in its purest form when even the light itself is dark. Or, as Brenda would have it, when the person's been absorbed by the body, identity fails its self-possession. But even this fails to penetrate my psycho-geography, the entire coastline, militarized for a transit corridor, water from Anatolia, water from Mesopotamia, it all ends up in LA. In other words, being *is* money, the conjunctive link of each relation thrown under the big wheel of ontology, which is my way of getting the sun into every line of verse, the fact that you can't see the goods being the only proof they exist. Possibility itself, like systemic risk, the caption beneath the photo reads "member of US kill-team poses behind dead body" resulting in my own evasion, this persistent failure to mourn, fodder for interminable sadness. As for the things that embarrass me most, I never turn down a free sample and my fantasies involve being fucked by day laborers, though these are arbitrary placeholders, little stages I trot out on occasion for performance enhanced tricks, no substitute for the thing I've been dying to tell you but still can't fathom. What will it take to arrive at so impossible an event, to lend positive content to the scene of that blank, a fossil of the future already lodged inside my stool. And what other feeling would be the right feeling to have when feeling itself has become obscene, the way open access buries these structural violations under the sign of love which, failing its calling to make something common [————], opens an empty place for this perversion. I mean, if you have the money, it's easy to privatize yr writing. It always feels good to feel wanted, like selling real estate with the hope that there will be someone to connect with inside the house. I'm just trying to be realistic without being naïve, so I go on touring the site, moving thru forests of unsingable delights, the trees along the perimeter expanding with the earth, while all my men get stoned on disbelief. This yields the system's waste, the only universal being the site of a redacted name, whatever refuses proper integration, anticipatory omen of a common place thus far only rumored.

PRELUDE TO COMMODIOUS

This is where it gets pretty personal hemmed in
- side acts enclosing sense eroding all my needs
For warmth & honey common phantoms things

Sing of use not being on our side they press again
- st my limit being a swarm becoming corralled
Inside the same nonsite falling to a cop's baton

Not failing the place property erases you see for
- ce shifting lines converging undoing time
The way we make it deep how deep the ground

Dreaming futures not being bound to rates rent
Open squares under private siege a coup
Like common sense undone the library itself hi

- jacked commanded dumped by armed pretenders
Say the commode goes up in smoke say what
You are has been revoked utopian imaginary

Say whatever you want has been unmade
& ready to be made again with
- drawn people arouse

> *— the place itself, this hole in the goods.*

FOR THE GOOD LIFE

This culture of the heart it's what I want
To give you an inflated idea of myself so
- mething unrecognizable or an image of it
Being this innate propensity of things

To be evasive I kissed his cock a bit he
Took umbrage broke my branded organ
With no future yr floating lines make me
Really hot like direct address there's al-

Ways a soldier getting off in the wings
Where nothing can come in from out
There except the words they keep things
Coming wherever new industry is wel

- come I keep digging for you to see
Time make my body delirious w/ trade
Whose skin fails to name whatever's in
It making missiles & houses for the good

Life equals what the army guys know
They're gonna snap but if I could
Only kiss a few more like you

                    — *my song might have real weight.*

THIS CELL IN MY HEAD, BEING MADE OF WAX

Don't talk of 'stages' cause I'm fucking co
- ld and frozen forms can't express the real
Force police equivalence development ground
Rent makes our mirrors the effects of more
Uneven tyrannies than the one they staged
Under other skies long ago spells no more
Than words I've said when the talk gets real

- ly monstrous more than what we love we do
In yr country I mean yr person where the object
Form of things becomes another self-reference
To the car I rent accruing industrious glamour
That's not ours to hold in you I've held some
- thing fashioning skin no bone remains a pool
Casts back yr image where no reflection waits
For me the calcified and hollowed sign my
Sleep's become until now unnamed as vision

When there's nothing more to see I think I've
Seen thru fog to a dark of such pitch the screen
Goes white with it so much light calls an end
To stages because things can't go on deve
- loping anymore resistance to regime
Being what one sees when one be
- lieves irrupts inside this hole
In what we sense

— I mean yr body in a tent, the sky.

NONSOUND, A MUSICAL

No song onsite these airs sing what things
Can't be needs forgotten grafted manes
To metal scored hews whose breath resides
In place where matter voided voices still

The things I've abolished beat down ears
With instruments plump dealers produce
Extracted breath by force returns tones
Sound silence dead in a cavity my mouth

Collects their parts in words bones graft
Lives undo deeds themselves struck out
Downed subjects don't matter by accord
Threat menace refuse no living sounds re

- sidues breath resides in anthem noise
Choppers ammo floods a sky not being
Sky and the sea's vast plains whose military
Sonics sew the ground what we produce

Trains ears on spectral sounds surround
Us systems sing in private mouths deeds
Force airs menace ears metal tones things
We've muted living hums blown bits into

Them being bone ash all our dead remains
Residual song refusing clings to breath
Wrecked mouths tubes absent horns beats

— silence onsite, a music we never hear.

INTO THIS SUSPENDED VACUUM

for John Wieners

Whatever militates against our dreamier pleasures I have
Become the same meaning utopia's crude petroleum jolts
Coded rubber heat singing things that turn blind eyes to waste
Erasing worlds being serial resolves my fate in theory I think

I want to love and loving kiss yr many addled hallucinations
Hunger fulfillment's no longer a glamour hangs dependence
On feeding the thing eternally expressing selves in public
Johns voices saying before you decide to leave me leave

Me a rag some hair a duct or mass producing anything external
Can't arouse thus corrodes the tongue with news I can't be
Warm or think my own repression cause it's too hot inside this
War to dream communications a soiled body nobody wants

To express can't be itself in goods another total embracing
Wants to believe belief enough to become the world we can't

~~– cause the cops can't fucking fathom.~~

The barricades were far away when the sinew of system's rule
Pit me up against my friend whose politics I'd suspected
But managed to avoid until the bombs began to fall. Ruined
Aftermath of monument lodged deep in my throat, the cubicle
Enclosed my tongue-splayed spectacle as it lay bare or bare
- ly consonant with itself while the alphabet, aroused & unwieldy
Expands the limit's extremity, the law now incarnate in the PD
- 's baton & shielded horizon where our bodies press the gown
A forced caress. So absolute a distance haunts this proximate
Closeness turning my feelings into gas, a sublime state. Or maybe
It's the other way around seeing how my GPS app tells me there's
Someone closer to my own location than myself. So our convers
- ation was void from the start, cunningly masked as common
Sense whose unfailing power the situation so perfects or perfect
- ly harnesses, the way the war has harnessed its own image and
Disfigures my voice inside each contemporary object, the poem

Where inaudible logics of death & expansion find hospitable
Repose. Whatever autonomy my writing falsely promises liquid
- ates in endless yearning, sweet sentiment of the dying world
I keep hearing about, dreaming of everyone I love turned back
At the line between 'free zone' and 'siege' like the tour guide said
In Sarajevo where unaligned forces once called for appeasement.
But that was long ago under Clinton when state sponsored human
- itarian aid was better prepared to mask the moneyed squeeze.
Would that I were only able to take revenge on my dumb interior
Whose squeezed interests here join strategic targets there, securing
My self or at least its image to a state of nature. That's a theory
Of personhood I guess. So I close my eyes and summon pictures
Of his body, getting off on these sad feelings. Bombs were falling
Already on [————] in accord with figures of justice whose
Congruity with public opinion produces plosive torsions

My syntax, unconvincing, the embarrassing tics, a social stutter
Masked by product or its negation as my skin breaks out in fabled
Currencies undermining each position, these zones of tacit agree
- ment, a whole archipelago of reason's debris dissembling more
Familiar forms of speech or a blank in the world system where
Every cry reduces to the known & measured, so dismissed.
Common places erode as quickly as they harden around
Disguised command, whatever promises to bring me pleasure
The ruin of money itself against whose pricing surface my poem
Assumes a form of emergency management, clinging to its private
Effects. Boys garnish dreamy signs withdrawn from use, the wound
Itself an index of event, this vacuole, my error, a gurney where the
Body lies. It's still unclear what meaning the poem conducts, how
One thing fattens as another lies prone for feeding. Just tell me
What square to be at now that all my friends are gone, like every

- one's sleeping off defeat whose premonitions haunt my gestures
In advance to parry the coming blow or at least not give in to it
- 's dumb reflex. Okay, the poem might fake a feeling or cop a feel
From which it turns to blush as familiar moves & vulgar meanings
Pool in excess of what makes my movements sing. I have a song
About his hair I'm anxious to sing for you, tho it'll have to wait. Yes
Carnage over there relates to obesity here, but this eludes my analysis
The way a detainee's own study in hunger hangs upon my fable
- d meat. Between human rights, force decides the way it always has
But my tongue, still splayed, makes me incomprehensible, a needle
In a dusty groove, his body coming back in a shipping box again
And again, tracing the routes of all my agile products from forest
And factory hewn as they measure my body's place and coin
- cide with the park, a riot in color & light, auratic haze, his belly
Riddled with holes, my pillow. A soldier's piss, warm broth in my
Throat, sweet digestif after the bloody fuck, wherever I can have his
Fire being where I'll have it. This is how I give myself away, naked
Before the other, a risk-adjusted exposure conned by branded terms

Joining spirit & bone, commonplaces I name myself the way a blank
Floats thru my verse, patient sinew of that spasm becoming song
The one I mentioned, being of his hair, I haven't forgotten it
His gentle fat whereupon I love to sleep, there being no reasonable
Utterance, no hope in speech without excluding someone I might want
To persuade, like you, or naming myself as one persuaded as if I could
Name anything true about my own condition whose appearance fails
The poem's perception. Being a hazy form of apprehension, my half
Awakened sentence can't bear witness to impossible voids [————]
Where the bombs keep falling and cries never cease. But even this
Arousal sings the failure of rational distribution as fantasy engulfs
My form, the impress of that absence, ruse of my wellbeing. Some

- one said the future lives lodged in the present's contradictions
Another vanishing moment disappearing inside movements of debt
Whose consciousness I find myself regaining on the toilet
Of a transatlantic flight, desperate for a form to help me manage
My feelings, conditions having rendered the friendship impossible.
Still, the poem has to side in a world that wants to subsume
Every side. I gotta say I'm astonished to be here writing to you
Without experiencing my incontinence as an effect of lousy
Planning, imprudent investment recalling the way I once had
To empty my bowels before entering that sex club at 1808 Market
With nowhere to go before paying the fee. But that was long ago
Before the city changed and my friends began fucking online.
Arguments like these merely function to affirm the most
Depressing triumphs of common sense confirming things
Already here, all our digits having become obscure prostheses
Of militarized event, vehicles of tinted flight before which I
Lurch from occurrence to occurrence, desperately
Making all these stupid calls

    — *to the dead in whom this dream will not come true.*

SNOW SONNET

So there's no more to arrange no sound
To sing returns the distance to our song
Decrees no proper names become poems
By force we're sliding back into time no

Command mouths these things that don't
Count we've born no issue nothing comes
Back from the tape the radio recorded us
Holding hands in one another's dusty ruts

Given no static voice whose shape our body
Equals nothing in this general issue weighs
What our empty bag proposes blooms no
Shelter and stinks of sweat theft bloody

As any free-minded broadcast fills arranges
The sky brings us here to tape these parts

– together.

RUMORED
PLACE

CONSIDERING THE SEX THERE

Rub this patch a little harder, he says, looking up at me ruefully from where the shag ends in a white deluge. My digits deviate, unequal to the task. Considering whose shit confirms the meaning of public space, did you come inside me, or were you there to begin with? All this gets cast in gunmetal, lodged in steel, a trace of history, or the radical need itself. There's not enough material to document so concrete an affair. Pressing my love into the pages of his holy book with fronds of creepers on Macau, better shirts'll be made here and then some table bunting too. How much like being dead, or being the leaves themselves. Spread good words around this organ, my lips in lieu of fish oil. Having become so absolute an abstraction, all our relations become obsolete before they can ossify. Our touch already connotes impossible worlds when we settle into playing hut. Row raw a little skinny in the pink. Cheap scraps of porn cushion the walls for public safety – grapefruit-sized lobes, unblemished flesh, spasming sucking sounds coming from the North, now give blond boy back his meat – as if all this were meant to turn away the dead. How the world turns too away from every word as wind-turns thru sun-turns and images of the camps forge collective memory in vats. Just tube the lawn, spray the patch. And so we go, and in going, he does things. Longing to be one with our Galaxie® whose metal time consummates a singular force. There's something out there, beyond this boundless drive. Being more immaculate than boutique water, more rudiment than fossil fuel. Constructing inside holes for better trading, collective futures in the stocks, all this deals in floating unities. Coming in the difference, exchanges thus expressed, he no longer spreads around. There's something not being about spending and what could be more dangerous than that.

THE WOODLAND SCENERY, HAVING BROKEN
WITH ALL OBJECTIVE LOGIC, ADDUCES SOME
CONSPICUOUS SIGNS

No infinities – more like endless links.
All this stills in looms. Beyond the strand –
a still horizon, sunk ends the baited lines
warp depths half-sown and strewn.

The total thing against which we rail
– being an immaculate cloud –
a huge complex web of lines and routers.
Something having not yet lifted

separates us from the place – a tab
of shabby darkness coming from the north.
Sounds like harvest time for the natives
Still not feeling much –

and there may be some anguish in that.
Lagoons sink under ochre skies – transverse
vibrations shifting west to east.
Pursuant to abandoned interests

the people here appear to be dragging
big old broken limbs or shanks.
Looming stalls. Settlements wedge,
remains in names we still can't trace –

from whence this force to bail our dying
industry – still busting up the place in stills.
Who went and slashed the mallowy dawn
Looking out on fields of bone –

•

picking up a bunch of lost whereabouts.
The entire sum of human relations
– fanned by gentle trade winds. Detained
in a car park where a fibula found, a pillaged dump

trenches full of personal effects –
silken thighs and lots of teeth. All this fails to correspond
to anything – trouble being some people don't think
much is happening unless you can see

a lot of suds. Blank expanse – the total expense
of getting personal about all this. Spreading
out to search the past for future parts
dismissed *en route*. A little hard earned cash –

purchase some primordial property – deep space
a mysterious work, becoming mealy sorrow
– personality, or any piece of admissible I.D.
Too late to acquire effective skills –

it's a bitch to learn the rules or feign a little
proper evidence in photo booths.
Following the recompense from Nuremberg
to Nablus – another formal opportunity exceeded

by its content. Turning up divisible pasts – reporting
"some strange emotion" upon seeing all this
piled inside a vault – the thighs, the teeth, etc.
– the longed for thing long gone from its interior.

Never had want so undone the shape of me as it did that night
when he posed this question on the bed. We'd often end up
in a little room like this one contains everywhere. Papered in
the pure lime underside of bruised. One night what I was
trying so hard to contain began to seep out on Geary Street.
A fluorescent glow it keeps this city down he said like a low
drone or hum. Subject to the weight of light we find ourselves
lingering on corners still unable to move. Like something
freshly flayed preserves the first incision there's no undoing
your name in me. Give me your wrist he says with a cuff.
Every other sound in effect resists something lodged in the
throat like a whack or a need or a subtile wreathe of haire. As
if there were no such precious thing just a wilting nosegay
some watercress or glue to prevent its substitution. As if by
running that blade down under where the flesh is soft you'd
suddenly see blood on yours. But he knew which of that
honeysuckling fever knew it for himself and showed me
wide escapes in tapes of future happiness. Your light is a cool
blush lost in what neon mist drifts in from the street. This
is all background for the scene I'm making absolutely like
he wanted me to see him and I him me. And so I'm walking
into that sex shop on 14th and Harrison he says and the guy
behind the counter all dolled up in plaids and spurs with a
studded collar you might see on any Fifi in France. Looking
at you I imagine a reliquary so many outward signs the advent
of future souls lost in latex and hide chips of bedpost or
bone. Like the real church we ducked into the little Russian
one all the way down Irving by the beach. Lying between pews
so anxious to be assumed. We were barely touching but I'd
known nothing more exquisite. Your light is blue from the
glass. The form his proposal takes already anticipates this
blank undoing. So we climbed the three flights same as every
night pausing step by step for you to catch breath. O starry
night. Come smoke with me he says from the fire escape.

Everything seemed to be 'going well'. A shame it's so small in here for one he says and places a finger above his eyes to drive the reference home. The conversation goes something like this without going anywhere. Your tongue strikes what space I fill completely with intimations of the impossible love. Possession haunts the little room like a vice we still can't move in. He'd like me to hang suspended between periods where our meanings suffer more than sentence. Space comes to naught there between a wrist and a post hardly room enough barely a yelp. And the bed too a floating surface or vision of ground to sound everything stable shifts beneath *this is*. Not the word for any thing not the hazy threat of a part of speech or me but the real untouchable it he frames. Or he it. Writing this now recalls an elderly Hasid who exceeded obligation in 1987 to procure for me a set of kosher phylacteries so concerned was he that I might leave the Old City unbound to some unspeakable name lost outside the only place from which to write oneself away and back again beyond what frontiers frame me. Borders are negotiable they say after periods of terrific struggle so does this one count like that. Names remain the same to ensure against all innocence. Call it body call it self there's always plenty more where that came from. Location concentrates a thick and goopy sap or resin. Nylon grafts the memory eye screws rush the carpal tunnel. I hear you calling still from every fire escape. A palm thru the window just out of reach. Your jaw is a floating habit I put on. Hands gesture toward me now phantoms limb like Catherine's at the glass or Carrie's up from 'neath the grave. Can't you hear them calling us. Now is the time for great listening. What wiggles like a worm deep inside my ass is a figure for what's eating you. His poem proves the world's untried virginity. Traffic moving out on Geary where we'd just been walking keeps time going counts cars like sheep. Beauty stills in murky pools when no finger parts and drags the film to one side. Can I tie you up now he asks crawling back in from our little *balcon*. Let us prove so entangled an affair bind it to the real world of wood and springs. Cased in glass like Saint Stephen's hand in Budapest or a chip of Mary's tooth. Little bits of dappled egg shell the vast and urban. Whatever he meant by it I can be that figure and fill what space expels me. Marked by a ribbon or the proverbial lock of hair in the story she leaves on the precise spot of assumption. That cues us between pews. Give me your hand to what wedded purpose crimps sensation like the little plaits in a torn dress awaits some stitching voice. That thread is nothing but the gash too. Oh but night time in that old bed in that old house and these sounds still transport all this up creaky stairs to where my father had slept at eight years old too and where my cousin in a moment of savage encounter born of weakness or an excessive taste for sweets tied me naked with the terrycloth sash of his robe to opposing bed feet when the old lady rushes in and I can't stop laughing. Snap the fuck out of it he screams and slaps me rocking like some autistic on the bed. Each touch returns like a sentence can't be parsed. Posts animate wrists. Thoughts spindle down from better brains than this compose you in me. He was gentle with leather. Power's not a metaphor he says whacking me with the backside of his hand and then quickly asks me if it hurt. A moan rimmed with teeth buried deep in gum mimes the only meaning. Why are you always reaching for your wrist like that. To see if I'm still here. A soft chew floats the room in a nibble where some I locates itself inside your mouth. So concentrated a location opens the flow in a bedpost or between. Where we be this brush this friction this abrasive rubbing of unfit worlds without which there'd be no fiction no love. His bedroom is at the top of a third-floor landing off a heavily trafficked stretch of Geary above the greasy spoon for breakfast. So we already know how the story will end over eggs and toast. Doubting the wood of what hurts most vague hopes for what lies beyond the bed. And this bit of string I wear around my wrist now that you're dead courts our still location. All your better-brained thoughts make a self of me your colony your swarm and archipelago. A finely twined shock of hair around your wrist can prove my transmigration. Not subject to the demands of light you rise through my shallows gone now all depth as you surface and spread. All this across a milky swath of skin mysteriously depilated into states of such expectancy. Or out on Geary you seep through in a gesture spill over in a word to some stranger. Where the sidewalk once conveyed us past ruined monuments and old hotels in Cairo and a brothel where the trade's pressed up tight against glass off which you'd have to peel his prick like a squashed bird didn't see it coming. Who isn't trying to glimpse the horror and still escape unscathed. Subject to the weight of what light protects us from the world of things. Bent over like an Elizabethan rake whose hose had fallen so low the mere stoop was enough to send me tumbling. You are my selfe I say before his back peels away to tuck me deep in furs. Wrapped in mink like Petula Clark on the cover of that record proves our sense of every warm thing. That's enough I scream trying to replay the sound in other mouths. Dawn barely cracks the concrete gray outside the back window the sound of bottles break on stone. Are we acting out a trauma of beginning or are we having fun. In a vase of dahlia and fern I can see when my neck cranes beyond the headboard our scene refracts like a stem cut by water a broken line or world. The room quivers in a wristing pulse arresting post slender channel through which a falling world falls. And you is all that exceeds me. Quartered by foreshortened limbs of wood I run away on. This knot of imaginary servitude on which I still depend extends your mastered province in every direction. Startled out of sleep by the sound of stones and glass. And since I could save none of you I let go more of me into what can't contain such want. Don't be so afraid he whispers and holds my night so tenderly. But I'm ashamed I can't perfect belief and choose the post instead a thing in which I cannot master doubt.

SITUATION, BEING ON A ROCK

The peculiar perspective of the sea in connection with the ground
we stood on gave me a complete idea of deluge.

John Keats, upon composing 'Sonnet to Alisa Rock'

. . . . and yet so tenuous in its hold on the status of 'event'
as to merit an almost complete invisibility in the guidebooks,
mirroring in this paradox the major occurrences
of the decade yet to follow.

Taylor Brady, *Microclimates*

And then the lines go dead and forge our inmost com-
position. Falsetto of the deep, it sounds like love, our crudely-
woven verdant warp. Anything to ape in lieu of meat. All
that's social slags above the shock and awe, the rock's white
shit, the sea fowl – all this being more than foul, more than
white and, taken for a posy, droops inside our gravest strata –
for thou art dead asleep!

Gaps in the intelligence, passing into being – the doze and
faze, a gilded lapse – a bald white vacancy – being the shudder
of some objective force – bound inside no agency – the
complete idea of a deluge – cinched in national brackets –
fucked there – detained, "and safely so" in containers – made
of Chinese steel – these articles of faith – where they were
shot – dumped.

Other assets passing thru intelligence – being is being detained – a value added to containers made of steel – national brackets eliminating each objectively impossible person, place or thing – non-financial transactions notwithstanding, whatever negates each challenge to production – palming off the waste on all the project effected peoples, or PEPs – being outside the space of true relation – their rock, it's nothing after all, mere blanking off the grid.

Disfigured gulfs expand, a hush inside detained – rings of unheard terror – a curious music spread across the glued penumbra – that's us expanding in the seafowl's screams – these skinny necks of land, molded into big fat states of being – monetary subjects with no cash at all – waving snapshots of our rock, the power plants and dams – containers made of steel, into which, the others, being hailed, summoned – shot, dumped – effectively implemented, buttered – sealed.

Forging gaps in multiples of ten – hundreds of thousands condemned to a similar intelligence – product of ungraspable forces – these ideas being our social phenomena – something having been, subtracted from the scene – erased between a femur and the bank – still producing in the hold – being is being this property – deep space, personality – again, the stocks, the cuffs, and – steel, the horizon beyond which our meanings cannot go.

When up juts this dumb rock – a concrete vision or motive for which no object stands in place – a gap where nothing can be – embedded, still invoiced – coming deep inside containers, the steel – in which all this shipped not long ago – where his chest ripped, riddled with the meat – floating to the surface, all this clings to nothing to cling to – still something moving thru all this – assays to forge the plunge around ourselves – a shudder passing thru intelligence.

Filling throats with so much rock – there being no such devastating thisness – no containers no steel no trench – mere mnemonics of which – echo before the thud – thrusting back intenser spume, spitting out great wads of it, as if we could ever parry such a blow – the pale white skinny – sinking down, a bony ash – no concrete evidence to substantiate the assets – no correct theory to account for what has taken place – this event now moving thru us.

This immortality of which we die in droves. Stumped on the line, dying just to feel the blank moving thru us. Being the jilt and chaff of all that will have been, kneading the voice into a vacant shape. Condemned to making art, its moment of realization having evanesced or having not yet arrived, our specious activities prove themselves wired to the thing's nefarious intent, rendering our separation from all this both true and false. Reconnaissance revealed the poverty of our methods and techniques to be necessary for getting some bare sign thru, but our objects and effects, still too deep and foamy, have been steadily disappearing from the documents, siphoned from the scene. Finding no chance operation, no arcane procedure by which to master the historical cause, we've failed to isolate a single extractable fact and our ~~powders~~ powers of description have been sundered from each attempt to explain all this. No longer being what once made television 'television' – real live action – we are crafting forms to keep these rumors of incapacity from clogging all the lines and routers. No one will want to read our poems after the war, and this speculation constitutes our hope and ranks there.

•

Struggling to throw ourselves outside the terms of all detection, our fantasies fold us inside havens of similitude. Pretending to be sensible, even popular and pretty, we dissimulate intent with hands poised just inches above the brow in studied gestures of incomprehension. More like Hecuba on the beach, there's something we remain unable to assert without becoming ill, and so we struggle to dispel the sickness, passing fits of foamy diffidence, busting up these crusts of desperation. We all want to hear similar voices, but those who do are detained for suggesting they'd entered some new paradise of communication. Finding succor in fields others have sown, even erecting huts there, we soften the accusation with a musical distance composed in simple tone rows. This allows us to elaborate a reliable notation, eliminate contingencies. Fugal variations, for example, are a strategic means to turn somnolent anxieties into a dilation of pure delight, revealing possibilities of endless discovery without ever moving forward. So we practice liquidating the chimera of progress in which a plenitude voids. The need to go beyond such principled inaction means risking our own abandonment at the site where all our friends were lost. So we replace this sentence with another proposition, positing "love cannot be risked", presuming it's still the risk itself.

•

But the event can't endure in time being subject to a void in perception. All this ensures the link between terror and some nameless joy. Rereading these lines and nearing despair, I try to feel the other thing moving thru us only to return, as if by reflex or lame habit, to the old lines and ritual question-naires, filling in our background against which these figures emerge and loom ("officer with Taser", "clubbed body inside a bag"). Collapsing on our sides without feigning the refined hat trick of so flattened an expression, we know our slogans will not unleash the antidote. After dreaming of the one who slays me, I only wake to find him dying of voluptuousness. Desire is a detour, but when love appears like a prompt on the screen, I still feel the stony hardness of the other boy's clothes. My femininity has been mistaken for some wily avoidance and so I'm left to bake, buried to the neck in sand, a head exposed for stoning, my skin turning into an undifferentiated surface inside the sedan upon whose fat upholstery we wake to find our bodies blackened by the recently laid asphalt. Ransom is subsequently rendered with ease, but the referent in whose debt we remain hostage to our very being has been floating unfixed ever since Nixon abandoned the gold standard.

FANTASIES OF SCARCITY UNDERMINE A
LOCAL INSTIGATION

and separate us from the place in having become it.
Lacking papers, missing proper forms of evidence
– arriving at a blank, it all goes

Busting up in stills – strung out on the lines
the routers – some promised place replacing
still suspended throngs – all this doesn't appear

to be happening here – as curfews smother sleep
secret benefits secure a purchased land –
our thoughts go freezing into pinnacles, jutting into sockets

a certain physiological dominance exerts control
over the less active parts – recalling something splayed
upon a table. Bodies foreign to our value system –

standing in for the absence of these signs – amazing
what a skin can go on feeling long after its conditions change

·

all this goes inflating with amazing sensation.
Staring down at the fifteen-year-old hustler's hard-on
– growing abundant with the pleasures of *this* world.

Scarcity within the nucleus goes on shaping
even this report about it – being just one example
of a thing recording the conditions of its own inscription

– picking up something coming thru a trench.
Having lost all sense of need or having lost the need itself.
What little space obtains between good public speech

and the old pornographic codes. Producing lots of skin
just to equal better sex in huts – I mean the real kind
like when the guy's not even there.

All this relies on a diminished referent
whose occlusion remains a function of both fantasies:
ten throbbing inches of rock hard stud

– or ten billion for a shield.

where once a history, now these collective fantasies of feeling
obtain. Maybe that's all it ever really was, he says, a residual
film of imputed consciousness linking skinny necks of land.
Personal reflection, this mutilating gruel. Craven still with
his limb in my mouth, siphoning trace nourishment from
what particles remain to be negated, this endless operation.
Digging deeper still for concrete elements, our loss has
been preoccupied. My recurrent conceits, achievements
conditioned by the apparatus itself, secrete a second film
or residue, before becoming nature. That's us inside some
corrugated flab waving pictures of the building stones, one
hundred little heaps, the girder scrap, as if there were some-
thing true still lurking here. Bits of cellophane, the macadam
and tin, what clings to our skin as we cling to this. It's as if
each temporal element were replete with its own affirmative
moment. Sensing devastation from the fringes of a lake, the
time of this conditioning and the horror in that. So where's
this rumored place, he asks, and I'm pointing out beyond the
docks, out to rock on the horizon as if the thing out there
were already in here with us, and I'm screaming *look there, there!*
beneath which our tenses buckle & our phrases all give way
to content we can't say. Unable to document anything but
my own mute evacuation, and failing even that. Rushing, the
emergent crowd, a thick residual effect, by turns indolent and
harried in which our aims remain embedded. Grace radiates
from my particle, and I extend this to you for use. Something's
reaching out to us from where the event will have taken

place, cohabiting with the present. Still unable to document anything that's happening, alluding to uneven strata in production, these fissures in coherence

thru which untimely things still come. Unlike this feeling of weakness, our radical need for these endless negations, the fashionable propensity *to prefer not to* is but a formula in the logic of my own inaction now expressed faithfully by the apparatus itself. I mean, I's my own little fuck, a little parlor prance, an organ strained thru too much concentration. Stressing frail attempts, whatever administers the limbs *can we call these actions?* no longer quaking like they used to. A radiant emotional response whose half-life suggests an imaginary extension of the present across all temporal frontiers, a slow decay that blocks the apprehension of its own conditions. The arm being but a thing for waving pictures, trying to recover some semblance of more heavenly movements. Modifying pressured contents in the structure of feeding, matter's been demoted to mere potential. My point becomes a limit where a fantasy of universal enfranchisement still obtains so long as she doesn't wear a veil. And me, I'm still vaguely imagining his kiss, a thing that'll never come inside my mouth where the tongue's held in place preventing sound escapes. And so the terror in this must be infinite, I think, an endless mediation. Having been advised to vary my figures, techniques prove useful to avoid attaching oneself to sanctioned locations, gaping where the buildings stood, anything to make detection difficult. That's me inside some woodland scenery adducing a few conspicuous signs, the shame in having to appear. Dredging proto-semantic slag from deader throats than this, distilling sebaceous extractions from one guy's carcass in the trench as if the blank were without history and not one of its effects. Just tonguing for a better price

---

---

in the market of ideas. That's the thing about history, he says, it translates loss to gain, netting an increase in knowledge alone, this melancholy science, amphibious, disfiguring what silence ends in us with the blunt sensation of gills. A density of touch grafting other organs here, his fingers come in vacant deeps. Whatever yr hand conducts, I think, just scoop me out as these relations calcify to shell. Turning away from the injury, tirelessly destroying everything purported to express all this. But in here it's all gone cell-like, skeletal. Eroding at incalculable rates of exchange, so many bloodless effects, or at least the appearance of that. He's the best, I think, how I'd love to do something nasty with him, get beyond the throat and really go places. But something's already doing this to us and we wake as if on a tarmac *in medias res*, waiting to be subsumed, the epic of its fingers, a purely formal void, like a public john where you can buy anything, lost inside our effort to channel all the history otherwise. Clinging to remnants of the things we've become, just imagine the small-est particle that can be negated. Is all this momentary and passing, or structural and lasting? I mean will the promise of becoming citizens be enough to keep them all productive? Even scholastic questions like these might prove necessary in practice. This is what he asks me in an effort to renew the relation, a civic-box in which to check yr personal content and leave it at the door. But a blank won't get me hard like you will, he says, when suddenly, two soaring megaliths fulfill the promise of our collective negations. This is the semblance of an event to which we're held in thrall, its history being all we can't perceive. As if by force of feeling

---

alone we'd supersede these contradictions in the general formula, making our asymmetric relations public, a shudder, disrupting all intelligence. Chances are his kiss won't take root, nor will any other asset. But imagine this ever-worsening scenario. Let the bucket-seated Galaxie® stand-in for the whole apparatus as it's failed to appear thus far. Even this relation's already obsolete. These phenomena secrete the very time thru which the general line proceeds, a residue like paving tar, the macadam or tin, another figure for interminable exchange, some imputed consciousness connecting skinny necks of land. Entering states of fixation or arrest, maybe in that public john, a roadside stall where you can buy cheap cigarettes. A series of delicately linked moments, each replete with its own erasure, each eclipsed by the dominant mood, the drains and flows. Still there's something moving thru us, something our categories can't compass. Ground to the smallest particles that can be negated, we take the vehicle down Third to the docks toward the city gates beneath whose arch (being the strongest form, though even this has persisted well beyond its usefulness) we're left alone to parse the national speech in fits of pique, our stammer. Out here *in situ* our action has no consequence. It's a place where no one has to be, he says, and hence no place at all. At least not dressed like that, I rejoin. So he slips into a little red peignoir and leads me by the hand to a heap of scrap adjacent to what all this has been referring to. His loosely pinned curls escape from a bonnet, a greasy wig and boots, the composite of which has been giving him this saucy look. These are impressionistic strains and mutilated airs in which love and despair lose all contrast. Preserving some of the old good faith in production, it's infinitely divisible, I say, this univocal demolition, feeling for the blank of our undoing where something will have happened, suggesting intense feeling, dissolving in a creamy languor. But you, you fix my visual arrest like a theorem never could. In a place

---

---

where time is not abstract but rather a material residue of the apparatus, it's all like film at this point, the cruelty of duration. My so-called innocent confusion, dry black throat of idleness, left condemned to designate several of these things at once, clinging to the old realism of places. Now it's you who's being ontological, he goes on, as if I'd been humping a heap of girder scrap, begging for more fundament, this sluggardness from whence tomorrow's harvest never comes. Look how even yr exhaustion's been efficiently organized. Trying to recall how a relation ossifies before becoming obsolete, calculating in the dirt. There's this strange habit of holding the tongue under the influence of certain words securing a site to which more losses will accrue. Even our partial objects can't escape the tracking device, be it poem or population, silence or money. We hadn't been conditioned to want it at first, but then something changed and will change again. Rumors of deluge perhaps, whatever fills the empty space in us. Under what duress are you imagining all this, he remonstrates with a denotation of power to the head, and I'm rocked a little fucking dumb. Or, as if running the blade down under where the flesh is even softer, becoming sore thru some untimely contact with history, a barely discernible shudder, a blank we'd manage together to remember, a time and a place where one will have remembered a time and a place. Recalling the abscess in every public good, this thing goes passing thru our names for what we still don't have the name for. To end these occupations and with them every trace of everyday life, only not in so many words. And what could mean terror more than that, he says upon grazing my thigh

---

---

with his tongue, installing signs of all this deep inside my ass just to routinize the need. Go ahead, return to need, if need you must, he says, as if even this had obsolesced with the triumph of demand. But our means remain impolitic, lacking identifiable ends, exceeding possibility, straining toward our own posthumous figures. And in this sub-obscure excite-ment, some strange organ emerges sensing the potential, as if all this or something else were about to realize [————]

DISASTER
SUITE

Wetlands and marshes slow.
But my poems, like *phynance*
– this accumulation of waste –

I mean this, you and 'the cranes
Like ships', they're relentless
– targeting flows, pipelines –

Thru which the silence, too,
Has slowed, tho it's still refining
– me, I'm down to prewar levels.

•

Over and above the market, I'm off trade
Now, without exchange means nothing
Like 'the dawn' has no commercial plot

Not belonging to itself, no value affirms
What goes unfounded this won't count
As one subtracted from prevailing orders

Of inclusion, a unit has no real unity
I mean artificially, difference just can't be
Spreading in a tree is not a rock, a bird

•

Ground cleaves to what the new sun hews
My real relations having flown to where there's
No work proves a boon & open forms absorb

This shit in my mouth we're a living effect of
Waste these synchronies of organization
And command (see I'm finally opening up

To you alone at the time of sentencing this
Not being ours with a wage you can live on
Value for time is in the hedge fund as I am

In love tonight means we're self-grounded in-
Dependent semantics call it a monetary circuit
Breaching spans of life whose measures can be

— *traded.*

·

Hush now you say my arousal
Threatens us a noise so end-
Less murmurs mauls these

Quiet bodies litter something
Vast and brave technologies
Produce the carcass as such

•

Missing in the count now counts as one
– counts as if one weren't already
Counted others missing being shows

One counting things we've taken states
Arms ears whose hearing's hulking mass
Can't hear the excess of our industry

– selling senses counting bodies we can
Lick these grids of recognition mangle
Things count what counting can't have

Been inducted into what this cant
Can't mean yr touch yr tongue the proof

– my body will have been this place.

•

This war
Of want
Says what

I want
To say
To you

Of dreams
Or need
We need

Not speak
To speak
Of wars

Of want
I come
To love

So late
To you
My lost

– marine.

MUSIC
FOR PORN

ENVOI

Having arrived at the end, what I've been dying to write goes on eluding me. This is how friendship assumes its proper shape around all the things I can never say. It's what my mouth wants to be, a hole in the present. To love like this in America is to lose from start to finish. But on our walk up 18th toward Diamond Heights, I finally get around to telling Bruce that I can't bring myself to say goodbye to Mark, I mean forever, as it's pretty clear I'll never see him again, what, with me about to leave for Michigan, and Mark in such decline, and Bruce says I have to try harder, which is the right thing to say, and I know he's right, but it all thickens in my head, crystal grey fog, like in Rimbaud's cities, you know, where men seek distraction under the light they make. My poems don't make more than the dimmest light, certainly not enough to see by. Sometimes it feels like rubbing sticks, and if what I really need to see in order to write what I'm dying to write is the thing the poems so pathetically illuminate, then I think I'd rather see the light go out. Darkness consoles, loosens my bowels, relaxes my impotence, but it can't undo what conditions my vision. I mean, as syntax becomes determinate in the organization of common sense corrupted love a whole structure of space goes on eroding at a rate in excess of the time it takes to compose my sentence where I become again the self I've become thru violent contracts. Look how I fortify this grammatical place, ducking into the same dark theater nite after nite, where I'm caught with a soldier's dick in my mouth by a friend responding to yr civil complaint. I'm afraid this is what I've made of my community, anything to claim our ravaged bodies from consuming dark. It all fails to correspond to any sustainable happiness, there being a terminal disjunction between the finished goods and the money available to purchase them. And now, as the rain keeps falling on this deserted town, my social relations cohere around all these militiamen I want to fuck inside abstracted huts where no one lives anymore. So I go on thinking about that walk and about this poem, how it goes on and on and on because the moment to realize it has become my job, my filth, a collective residue, a thin film or integument that hardens around a body interred behind the wall, or buried in the yard, where it goes on secreting the mystery of my well-being. Real intimacy, impersonal as porn. I couldn't even tell you his name, though a string of phonemes I can't pronounce fills my mouth like his dirty ejaculate, or glue. These words keep me from recognizing him as a person, the proper name being a generic dysfunction that brings us together only to shatter us again. Even the shame I feel is waste. Being nothing more than fealty, this concession to appear if only to dissent for the other guy's pleasure, it's a simple effect of summoning having less to do with ideology than with my allergic response to being tagged, a common ritual triggering disgust, which like rage or ecstasy, were it only better organized, could bring the whole fucking system down. What I mean to say is that it's a risk-adjusted performance, all the bodies yet unburied, failing to coincide with themselves, a scene of permanent displace-ment, this hygienic bundling, my person, a quotient or lubri-cant, like liquidity, anything to make the organs useless. Each syllable strung like a bead on a rosary, inserted and teasingly tugged, one at a time, out the hole of my ass. Tickle me here with yr tongue and watch me writhe, the pleasure is excruciat-ing. Like any obsession with what appears self-identical, this sentence binds me in thrall to conspiring forces. Being made of iron and linen, asphalt and glass, my imagination dissem-bles a soldier's fat, and I get hard just thinking about his hair, completing the circuit of my autopoiesis. Still, there's transport in the body's vegetable existence. Even to have one's name cancelled, stricken from the general roll, demands a witness. Will you be that for me? Resurrection or theft, I'm thinking, as though it were a choice. Many incalculable intervals pass, during which I cling to ghosts of what impossible future haunts the present. Were I to touch the hole in his chest, a spontaneous surge of meaning would suddenly spring to life inside my own incongruent material, the spirit and the beef. Too many voices, can't distinguish my tongue in the mix. In other words, whatever use might promise has to begin with its critique, anything to feel the antagonism and not its consensual suppression. This would be the place in the story where Bruce asks me about the figure of the soldier in my book and whether it has some bearing on my intimate life, or whether the soldier's merely an abstraction is the flesh real? And I'm struck by his manner of asking, by how his question is just the question Mark would have asked, with the same clarity and concern, uncertainty and skepticism, and I recognize this as being full of implication, both for me and for the writing, even as I formulate my prepared response. Occupier of my inner world, a swan, having escaped its cage on the banks of some uncomely flow, polices my utopian longing like a military mimesis of the mind and expropriates my feelings in whatever way it can. Maybe this is what Oppen means by 'viviparous', being forever fucked by the thing we're wedged too deep inside to even posit as an object of our own sensation, there being no 'out there' anymore, determinate force having made no mensch of me. What happens, then, when the thing we need to see in order to know ourselves is a corpse withdrawn from view, and when even the language denoting that body has been buried in a classified autopsy report. Being, this spectacular production of absence. But I get off knowing I can at least relate to invisible suffering, lend it some semblance of voice, and then eat the thing of which I sing, filling my depth, feeling common notions stirring, lost in this vessel of exchangeable options. It's always the skin that vanishes first, then what remains, the bone, the ash, and I watch the erosion with perfect equanimity, an effect of everything looking so fucking small up there where we all disappear in larger systems. I heard Verizon is going to refund data charges on my phone, and for a moment I'm feeling sort of happy about that, but if we only could explain the survival of the working day as an accepted unit of economic measure, well, then we might be getting somewhere. As if my poem weren't already yr own blind glass, wedged like a slice of life between the gaping lips of my open cunt. Where ornament shatters, I return the message, listening to the stars for what will never come thru. I mean the soldier, he's my sick muse and deserves more compassion than I appear to offer, but he's already hardened into allegory. Standing in for a blank we can neither fill nor consume, the only thing we share being what isn't here to share, and the promise of that commons. Faking our most sensual relations with wage-slaves around the globe, then harvesting their earnings for warmth. Jerking-off onsite, I imagine a hot day laborer using my shirt to wipe his jizz, then my hand to wipe his ass. Producing appetite thru forced withdrawal, I marvel at the thing's capacity, a magnitude of failing grip. From somewhere deep, waste returns, my constant theme, this decay of sound, a wall of pure significance, the way capital flickers in an Afghani's wound, hedging our implausible intimacies, materializing my love. Identity being at once realized and negated in the soldier I sing of, whatever hope remains remains mediated by the same defiled corpses. Taking note of repetitions, I find myself treading the same terrain. Here comes that stump again, this time sutured to my elbow. As for porn, the fate of bodies constructed by money and the potential disruption of this fantasy. What counts for evidence as the debt ceiling falls on a naked jib. Someone speaks of the collateral necessary to keep the house, driving a wedge twixt life and speech. How my poems drown in murkiness between the twain. Gauged in fabled currencies against the going rate of meat, each new line measured with the spiral of value & profit connects with something deep inside, residue of the old resolve, my mucous, a post-industrial laminate on his cock. Let's lend a name to realer sensations, the feel of finance coursing thru my veins, anything to elevate the nearly unrepresentable limits of the world-system to the level of sense, or to live the positions we already inhabit as the practice of undoing them. There can be nothing more behind what I'm writing, I mean, no one has experienced this event from beginning to end, though the condition is hardly new. So I've assembled the following discreditable models, jerry-rigged mock-ups of a liquidated tense, negations of abandoned futures, making use of what I can. Rocky lowlands, marginal wood ferns densely covered with golden fur and rarer lichens brought in from the island, bind the world to theologies of labor, all the cotton gins and pharma-ceuticals. Upon being hailed, I'm completed by the sudden awareness of my own hideous shape, all feeling dead at the base of my balls. But behind the veneer of these earnest comments lies my excrement and cum, gross product, this residue of debt, cruddy yield thru which we seek transit, a justice in excess of any legible demand. Whereupon I wake with visions of the prison house, abattoirs stationed along peripheral fades, exquisite creatures of social waste, and all the things I'll never see that make me what I am. That's when Bruce reminds me that history is this series of discon-tinuous shocks connected by the sinewy threads of our own narrations, our friendships and meeting places, but I can't stop thinking about Mark, the way he'd question these poems and how I love him for that.

SOME SPECULATIONS (AFTER GEORGE OPPEN)

Like boys birds leave no hope
For anyone to sing or say all this
Isn't real it can't be happening

Such certainties of doubt we have
Fashioned ourselves out of things
Penetrate me like the nail does

Wood the skin secures its ~~rupt~~
Raptures verities time being full

— of what we've failed to make

•

Being the hidden starry life our language hides
What it can like any body would and dreams
A politics as if whose history has no future

Perfect losses we can't mourn what we have
Erected structures voiding space things that will
Have come inside no place being where we live

A fantasy of home secures their missing limbs
My cock ensures them tender organs fulfilling
Orders of state when they migrate with no bodies

And even more flexible forms

— this 'achievement of the housed'.

•

But for infantry you've offered
To hold my hand & in it
Place the name for something

Else say clarity for darkness say
Ditch for house or sky
A whole world in exchange

For foxholes and poetry
Equals this one defeat being
In the future perfect meaning

— you will have been already dead.

•

— now refer to house arrest

When yr home radiates my longing to be fucked
By prosthesis of that other sky say the boy or his leg
Blown away by contracts this fact being endurable

Becomes the unendurable engine singing of hygiene
And glamour being good but how lonely the nail
His palm the fingers my asshole leaves little

— hope for doubt.

ARMIES OF THE WOUNDED

So come again my troops no
- iseless mists vapors gather
Round me boys phantoms all

Fragments of a mobile space
Seared with our metaphysics
Of service & reserve the sold

- iery loves me trading what
The war heats up it offers
Worlds of feeling very deep

Much deeper than defiance all
Slain things being equal wealth
Bodies fucked real deep inside

– the nation's gorgeous booty.

•

My soldier my odalisque my
Fossil of trade pressing thru
Yr face an explosion of sense

Penetrates skin a landscape
Itself a catastrophe blowing up
A head somewhere inside

It being this dream of life

– coming in my hotel bathroom.

•

Nothing I can see from here equals
His impossible form all riddled w /
Their holes & pasted viscera travel

Far as value lives inside the dead
Things tagged a skin becomes this
Organ my hand moist intimate

— recess.

•

Following close upon his body
Parts stuff the marts of wealth I
Get moist for friendship means

All these guys ignite my love
With objects parsing lands them
- selves sleeves a soldier dumped

– his dead in me.

•

A badly dubbed audio his lips
Arouse my skin a canopy a sel
- ving sleeves inside a frame

Contriving recovery it's so patriotic
Duty crushed a head in my groin
Puffed up on the unidentified

Airs nothing real no experience
To speak of nothing to sing
These poems just keep coming

– this disease of my mouth.

MY OPERATIVES

War yet shall be, but warriors – are now but operatives.

Melville

Now that I've addressed the soldier luminous
Flesh all erotic mastery an anvil-din a wholeness
Comes upon me in this moment's dull emergency
A blank in the social fabric a police action now

Gone missing sanctioned with the halo of event
Open rents whose spirit pisses peoples my own
Shattered aspect jumbled shards fly valued dress
Dolled up the coded elements lift me even higher

Gestures fly yr fisticuffs lend identity a pounding
To all our dutiful goods how can we not have this
Paranoid relation to the names themselves eternal
Things screw truths into such stunning parks let's

Go there holding hands and touching even more
Than every soldier names us out beyond the war
Perception's reach I mean I'm the war's perception
What can't be heard inside me calculations of caloric

The only real event this thing impossible to prove
Took place & goes on reaching for me my history
Being one of these different ways of killing things
To access what my body's become yr private waste

Exquisite feeling hard clots sound the ministrations
Unsanctioned activity diddling more than ever now
Various and vague designs pump meaner things up
In our lung sacks as if other worlds were nigh whose

Common forms remain unseen to bomb her baby
This will have secured me here

— still longing for yr hair.

•

Now that we've undressed the soldier all my
Damp embarrassments sticky limbs stuffed in
Sacks his poor thing triumphed in an afterglow
Of poverty and shame a mutilated blank opaque

He's crapped spread eagle reveals what others
Refuse sells more events bigger targets dumps
Fail to happen precisely onsite is nowhere some
Ghostly void or dead zone around my body

Collects a hyaline film and my mucous hardens
Yielding new sugars upon decomposition sordid
Shapes assume their own lost objects memories
Of his hair the old gunner stained with eosin some

Thing they call experience for lack of any other
Idea of what happens to bone under war stress
Cathects yr thinking to my song twists love's
Caresses yearn to correspond with what destroys

Identity's torn apart so it's catastrophe that holds
Us together now that we've suppressed every other
Unexplained abused convulsion the very acts we
Disavow some things do happen addressing boys

Ourselves allows me to make believe I still want
My nudity neat absolute without value our skin
Contracts inside any residual content a filmy gloss
Of chemic aims splintered elements yr own

Oppositional remnants wasted turds scarred even
This holds my tongue inside yr immeasurable

            – gulf to be defiled.

•

Now that we've caressed the soldier I can finally
Touch myself again begging to be called the names
He used to call himself when the nation loved
His bloodstool eating it and fucking them singing

Is it in yet yes yes you can do it in the barest light
Of reason where cruel names find proper realization
And what you wear is how they eat little over there
Where the land is one with its things & peoples don't

Make me yr fall guy he said *I am you* when it's dark
Our own failure to happen is the only event worth
Noting phases sucking off a self-defining absence
Of content can't you see I'm already my own worst

Formalism all the marrow sucked out of everything
Lick yr own wounds it said as if the words would make
Me one with the current traumatic neuroses of peace
That's how we live on waste he said crawling out

Under the dead weight a carcass had come rising
When he saw me on my knees his dick in my mouth
Creaming him crushed beneath the weight of nations
Lost thinking what will this joy do to my tongue how

Will I call things back now this is sadness my friend
Bob calls it the unbearable sorrow of having no future
In the present and tho he had something else in mind
I'm thinking

— about what he said now.

That a body could be a real frontier. Strewn in fields of waste, organs sensing under siege, mere shadow cast of value, a hardened rind, or money form, whatever remains when you stop believing in it. A false membrane, a whole catastrophe of skin, the thickness of these accidents. One small annulus, a floating hole in *phynance* radiates my longing to be fucked under soldier's sun. Now's the time, he says, humping hard my thigh, dreaming the coming reign of poverty and love. There's ground for what this can't contain, yr swollen excess, gummy extension of a self rising like a hand from sand and slag, a glassy pink appearance, a hyaline veneer, looming just above the mouth. Feeding on pure product, poems and esoteric securities, harvesting my little field of corpse & shit. Crouching on the overpass, dreaming tight schedules of outgoing cargo flights, smuggling weapons to a desert in Chad. Cunning plans to colonize the dead, these feelings I'm still marshalling, tender affections harnessed to a hole between bad information and its real registration on a body I'll never see go down. Long before his brain's pronounced dead, I hear the thing has already occurred, so I visualize his innermost organ, this impression of truth, the signs that bloat his swollen thing. The landscape delinks me from every trace of physical trauma, nothing to reverse this unbearable lag in my productivity. Whose paranoia tastes like real meat anyway. I'm a mere police operation now, taking charge of biosphere and mulch, no services left to support our secret plan. But we've been very busy, harvesting the cup-like ascoma, so bulbous at the base, wondering how to transport our new object into fields of visionary prospect without turning up on screen ourselves. If I could only anatomize the sovereignty that's made itself continuous with a body language has all but abandoned. Instead, we work undercover in the cool aluminum shade, anodized, shot-penned and learning, still learning how to throw the simultaneity of these synchronized measures (differentiation, correction, punishment, waste) on a linear axis, plotting whose enjoyment of all my body's functions. At this point, anything will do to advance our counter-purposes, the secret of the thing being that it has no secret.

•

I can't fantasize about hot sex with soldiers the way I used to, and this is taking a toll on my writing. Gazing out on fields of prospect and demise, acknowledging old tree lines with perfunctory nods, barely tracking the thing beyond our diminished capacity to relate, my body lost inside the strudel of that thicket. Like a bag of shorn digits, it's all so supersensible. I run off with one and insert the thing fully, wondering whether I'll feel anything at all when I locate myself inside the dollarization of Ecuador and Peru. Feeling only phantom now, an inconsolable figure, a soldier's precious organ, a recycled impression on my processed affectionate core. I'm nothing but this raw material for military use. Otherness always resembles me a little too much for there to be any ethical possibility. The best way to end an occupation, he says before halting, as if about to divulge a deep secret, preparing his tongue to gratify all my needs at once. Yr delusion of mastery bears stains of my traumatic senselessness. Let me be yr tranquil erosion, the economy's vanishing causal force. Even after swallowing his piss, I still see myself everywhere I look, a series of seemingly endless grammatical subordinations, circling the withdrawn violence that structures the limits of our perceptual field, a blank in my own dislocation. It's a beautiful place and extends in every direction, said my soldier with no hands, and I imagine his prosthetic up my ass. Elbow deep, I love the feeling, and quiver with pleasure at the thought of being so near the goal. A fragment of mobile space, truer than the whole that's false as the sun. This fantasy keeps my delusion far from what terminus over-codes all movement in advance. I, being where his blood's no longer flowing, or where the shipping lanes cross. There's a structure of hierarchies embedded in this feeling, a whole spectacle of surface becoming sentient, my functionalist metaphysics. An anarchy of symptoms soon emerges as a self-enclosed order of signs and I kiss the hole in his chest, anxious to feel some semblance of a self inside any cavity whatever.

•

Pronounced dead, a soldier becomes my disappearing act. The consistency of the situation hangs on the body, being a hole around which everything that appears appears to cohere. It's a spell that holds me in thrall, unable to distinguish my proper subject from one deceased. Being what the language doesn't want me to do, the decision to *autopsy* all US war casualties helps the military eliminate equipment flaws by improving a fleet of crash test dummies. Whatever words exist for this fall apart at such a stunning rate as if to protect the value of each identity, parceling properties before they sell. Caving to these demands, I masturbate to fantasies of day laborers fucking me in the shadow of the screening station, a checkpoint beside the border's river diversion system where they're reinforcing old security fence before it can deform under a migrant's weight. I can't get hard enough for intercourse when the moment is sweet, but as soon as he asserts the fundamental right to liberty and happiness, being what my soldier has sworn to protect, I fall on my knees, take his member in my mouth, and beg him to discharge. Whatever shame I feel in the face of sovereignty is inseparable from this arousal. In a world of love and domination, sex becomes monstrous in just proportion to the monstrosity of that world. The skin, an endless organ of excitement and abuse, my own private pleasures being mere adjunct of that. Don't confuse this sentence for a proposition. Time itself, having already become a hardened artifact of the system, renders my orgasm co-extensive with the demands of production, but this is neither true nor false. In other words, time is a fighter jet, the way spirit is a bone, and the object of my rage secretes the same auratic halo. Like the best philosopher, my soldier subtracts the real from what can be thought and this enhances his allure, makes me love him even more. Translated into military language, the point is not to shoot, but to clarify the shot. So precision bombing has penetrated my poems and yet not even a single one of my feelings is precise, the words even less so. Put another way, the self is a coin. And while a soldier's corpse may be the limit of my world, his cock in my ass remains a vehicle of transport, the light by which I write this sentence, whose sense defies the stars.

OBSCENE INTIMACIES

Against this backdrop of total
- ity figures having found re
- lief as I have in my bowels

So bloated with event who
Walks away from it as I do
Having walked away from

Theater the barnyard filth
And debris lodged down de
- ep in soft tissue his severed

Genitals flown wider still
Shored against ruin gaps we
- deged or driven into being

– there being no deep inside spectacle.

•

My soldier died last September hit
By Taliban mortar while trying to fix
A tank tread his father feeling the boy

Had been murdered by insurgents
Wanted to see the post-mortem report
To verify other accounts he heard a

- bout the 24-year-old's death so o
- ffer comfort I say to myself say
The reservist died instantly when a

Hot piece of shrapnel tore thru the boy
- 's flak vest into his chest before break
- ing in 2 w/ 1 piece lodged in the left

Aorta leaving the other piece lodged
In left lung a mute & uncomplaining
Sleep being fatal form his figure

– my decaying dream.

•

One soldier returned in a state of decom
- position so severe that viewing his body
Was impossible only 3 days after his death

Being bio-ruin's outer ring what horizon
Whose sensation my rim a negative imprint
The world image collateralized risk mech

- anism a current military procedure to pack
Fallen soldiers in ice then transport them
To US Air Force Base for a 3 step process

1) Identification which includes DNA dental
& fingerprinting, 2) Autopsy and 3) Preparation
I.e. embalming the body a proper mortuary

Facility were one only in place over there
We'd have been able to say our goodbyes
But the boy was not

— even refrigerated.

•

The body appears to have been
Dead some time under a spell a
Dream nation water hood flex

- cuffs minor abrasions sub
- galeal hemorrhage bilateral
Frontal regions of scalp intra

- muscular hemorrhage of an
- terior aspect & nothing internal
Evidence of trauma scant

Cause of death indeterminate
Toxicology report negative
For alcohol and drugs I long

– for where yr pleasure lies.

•

My vision being a soldier's body found
In the brush of an extremely rough area
A training region near the land navigation

Course the terrain covered with trees
Brush area temperatures in the mid
To low 90s when the boy went missing

In a place heavily laden with creeks &
Drinkable water though it remains unclear
Whether this one had any water with him

And when his body's found rose-robed
In dazzling immortality it's unclear how
Long he had been dead there being

No sign no indication of any attack it is
Devastating to lose any soldier but this
One was a model soldier always looking

For the next task to complete his last
Status update *gone for 2 weeks so hit me
Up later!* before the body turns belly

Up in the rising sun

                    – *my sunk extinct refulgent prime.*

•

O leprous corpse monster of life
- 's waste killing suns for time
Being nothing left to see show

Me the secrets of matter & why
Yr blood's not my blood yr shit
My shit expelled into the same

Void & why yr cells yr tears are
Not my cells my tears contract
- ing nothing concrete wounds

Being nothing but this language
For a soldier's rush toward the real
- ization of uselessness

— sire of our common strain.

I've been told it can take years before one is able to grasp what one has written. I still don't understand a book I wrote called *Rumored Place*, so unresolved and in flight from itself. That work concludes with a blank or a bar [————] *placeholder for all we can't perceive haunting all we can* like the mark of something withdrawn from sense, which had migrated thru my book, a floating caesura separating visible and invisible *logic of porn* audible and inaudible *aesthetic of state secrets*. *Music for Porn* emerged rather feebly in that blank as my writing began to seek the shape of what could not be felt there, the content of that form like the plenitude of a void.

The poems whose music issues from this fault in perception *constant interruption* were seeking *groping* a figure, any shape or hieroglyph that might animate the contradictions *near perfect correspondence* between personal life and the regimes of representation *property and selfhood* that mediate my intimacies, be it to the bodies I love or the countless others withdrawn in scenes of conflict and catastrophe and to which my body is joined thru flows of arms and money, bodies I'll never see but whose lack of being *over there* has been contracted to my well being here.

A soldier keeps repeating myself. Disjoined from the world of values whose extension he is, he appears in blank erotic haze. Like an emanation, he emerges in a fault running thru militarized common sense *extension of my body* which he so spectacularly realizes. His appearance and reappearance won't quit, like a skip or a tic *symptomatic spasm I can finally feel* a figure I am only able to contemplate now *as if for the first time* and whose seeming centrality to my book is a consequence of this slow accretion of sensation, not its reason. In other words, the soldier is a phantom synthesis *artifice, fake* a cause summoned by its own effects. Check out how I fuse my attention to his form *this fault in judgment* as if his form had been present from the work's inception. But the soldier is not a concept, certainly not an original one, though he may be an allegory *mirror of ideology, from which there's no remove* a blank that both arouses and frustrates my longing for a livable world, at once portal and obstruction.

It's in the fault where I first encounter my apparition. The soldier appears at a remote sentry near the river, dripping wet, shivering, and clad in nothing but his headgear. He appears shaken, the light of worlds in his eyes, genuine in every way, though still able to walk it off. The soldier appears confused, if not demented, while bearing in his arms my own half-dressed and lifeless form. He appears to have been shot by security forces, his head shaven and with a slight beard, wearing traditional gray, loose fitting Afghan salwar kameez clothing. Dressed up in an orange jumper and green anorak, the soldier appears with his hands tied, legs spread eagle. He appears to have been trussed, but he's helpful at first, his limbs sun burnt and mighty, his thighs like great military engines capable of wielding the heavy weapons themselves. Like a comic strip character, the soldier appears and reappears, again and again, his features amplified and distorted like those of the capitalist, the worker, the terrorist, his head shaven, with a slight beard, wearing nothing at all but a bit of traditional loose fitting camouflage, his particularity being no more than a type, unclad and yielding, nothing but his headgear, lasers coming from his eyes, sublime music from his core. Despite being held at gunpoint with his hands tied, trussed and moaning, he appears to be healthy, no trace of the fabled powders in his stool. He can barely contain my rage, his fear, this love. He has a hard time remaining erect, and no longer comes at all. Again and again, he appears and reappears, shaken, capable, genuine, confused, sun burnt and mighty thighs, generator of magnificent light in which I find myself distracted, my head buried in his crotch, or his in mine, a sentence from which we might never emerge. He appears to sense me in a similar state and, even though I'm now lodged in a safe house down the road, far from the current unrest, I've been made pregnant with his child. There's no evidence at all, nothing but a feeling in a limb I can't locate, an organ I can't name, but the soldier appears to want me, or rather, he appears to sense how we're both in the same condition, taken aboard the same flight, and I immediately love him for this reflection of my hollow impression, love him as myself, a song I can't sing without singing his.

As my poems begin to stir in the fault, the blank [————] recedes and in its place there emerges this phony apparition *fragile appearance* which seems to sense *materialize* a fundamental convergence *interpenetration* of private intimacies and public attitudes *pleasure and surveillance, affection and war.* Value clings to the soldier like self-preservation *a film of cash, relation of no relation* betraying my love for the death drive. This is how history succumbs to natural force, which erodes its stable meanings with implacable puissance as they incline toward ruin and waste. My soldier is no match for this, he's too real, being capital's proper corpus, extension of its management and concern. Still the soldier has a hard time not exposing himself *his member* as caricature or parody. As if to parry history's blow, he appears like an allegory of contemporary decay, dislodging word from meaning, driving a wedge between costume and life, subjecting even the most reliable of all appearances *his own* to the dissipation it is his function to forestall. This is how a transparent appearance *all buxom mass and sterling girth* becomes my gross opacity.

But my soldier, he's allegorical by default because whatever language there might be to denote his corpse does not exist in the public sphere, so there's no other way to sustain a relation with that phantom synthesis over time. Appearance and value are rent asunder in his beauty *this chasm in sense, an emptiness that's killing me*. Having cut himself loose from the social relations that make him what he is, his figure stands in for universal profit. His body, my dissipative structure, a temporary life form, or species of provisional order *like a poem* conditioned by a state of ever increasing disorder, but whose ephemeral aura assumes the function of something secure, something constant, something fixed. Sensing its own decay, value clings with fierce tenacity to the very things *bodies* that will be sacrificed for it. Just as he disavows the debauchery of capital *whose servant he is* my soldier becomes evermore debauched *sinks below the hemisphere of sense, as I might sink my nose in his ass* down along the precipitous fault of old imperialisms. With the militarization *financialization* of daily life, lyric is caught up in these same abstractions *value credit debt* as overproduction penetrates the soldier's body and weds it strangely to my own *radical discontinuity of flesh and world that the poem longs to bridge.*

Hazy eros *residue of money* hovers around this figure, and settles on my skin. I can't wash myself of its thick condensation and my poems have lost that apotropaic power to deflect the soldier's image, to keep it from usurping my own whenever I gaze in the mirror. The poems want to feel something *buried improvised device* to destroy this reflection, anything to activate whatever improvisation will have to have occurred here in order for tomorrow to be other than today, a future that fails to resemble the ongoing accumulation and privation that constitute the present. As part of an effort to ensure its claim on false futurity *extension of dead time* the present resurrects a fantasy of meaning *identity* that animates the soldier's figure like a ghost *money*. No doubt, Melville senses this in "A Utilitarian View of the Monitor's Flight" when he identifies the modern soldier *circa 1862* as mere "operative," incarnation of the hoary warrior, who, in yet another manifestation *today* will become a prosthetic of finance, a tomb of meaning *never there to begin with* as it becomes one with nature.

And just as nature abrades the stone, history abrades *revolts* its most constant forms, denying them of all but the most transient meaning, revealing the transitory bent *hallucination* of historical significance. At the same time, history, like allegory, formalizes the erosion of its own meanings, generating signs for that which bears no visible signs. This is how capital organizes the imperceptible relations that make our life-world a function of the abstract and fungible *infinite exchange of bodies and things* identifying the human corpus as but another limit to move beyond, "to dump your gorgeous body, now deceased / where the other garbage goes" [Baudelaire].

Soldiers, sex, and money: things toward which an allegorical imagination inclines as it grasps a form wherein a plenitude of meaning *value* coincides with its own liquidation. Nature hardens in the money form *whore's make-up, soldier's thighs.* Appendage of finance *most allegorical of capital's regimes* the soldier assumes a place beside that of the prostitute in whose body intimacy and commerce exist for each other. Vehicle of exchange and pleasure *receptacle of cash and cum* the soldier's physique arouses and neutralizes the relation between money and life, just as he eroticizes technologies of control. Constructed by money for the protection of money *social relation as death* he lacks the very thing for which his figure has been assembled. His sold hole bears the stain of my overproduction. In other words, my social alienation may be completed in the body of a soldier, and so in loving him I can finally love myself.

Today, the US soldier's body becomes a perfect pornograph when it's a dead body *casualty of finance, guarantor of my pleasure* a body whose image has been legally withheld, removed from public circulation, just as its autopsy report has been classified in order to preserve the values that body died for, values transfigured in the soldier whose hard muscle materializes our common resource, first rendered as sacrifice *purity of waste* and then withdrawn from view.

[————].

DISASTER
SUITE

It's nothing but doctrine poetry distorts
The things we live among and I can't see
My use of force and the housing question

May be as real as what an anti-social poem
Looks like this when the wind veers in para
- phrase we all fall short of hair-splitting de-

Terminations singing gulf streams heating
Arctic slipping icecaps saluting a meter of
Sea level rise and though I lack good stimulants

My commune lacked good ideas large scale
Production small things too but all that
Failed so let's make love like poems devo

- ted to doctrine distortion realer subjects

                    – all withering disinterest and reaction.

●

These sounds control a public sphere where there's no more
Public no place uncontested nowhere to caress my stick in you
Can be the dove I'll be the agent of my own liquidation I

Dreamt a conquistador & his top ground meat cruising aisle
Eight singing I want this one skinless that one on wheels I hear
Myself saying as we scuffle along so hedged about by social

Technicians of my utterance adjusted claims hooked into
Speech being full of minor incidents all contested spaces sort
The rules of place enclosing units transcendent words go

           – the way property threatens those who'd rather picture.

•

After the war let's forget about sex and go on
Back to loving the way it could've been
From the beginning when words were good

We had cash in hand and a cool way of thinking
About fuel and light we denounced fake problems
Beautiful perversions connected with gas the danger

Being some fantastic annihilation by explosions
At our own selves' hands selling futures
Markets being the honest way of arresting life

Goes on clinging to smut which makes it all pretty
Nice and sad when there's no one left to piss on
Me and our arms pawn time in local munitions

Dumps our waste in useful shares can we still
Say these things think in private equity I means
Someone who can distinguish what looks good

And what's dead as command becomes the good as
Such no time clocks to punch when the firing blows
In here I'm still clinging to disaster being such

A strong man erect I mean I could hug them all

     – ungrievable bodies all covered in shit.

•

Ejaculating in terror, he wore my uniform and talked
Real big about our transcendental subject
A corpse in Gaza, another Suprematist painting

My *aeroplan* of purity and shame where I find myself
Wanting realer things, sewage sweet to help our dead
Boys realize better options, peace and aid

   – the mind to languish fully in its shadow.

•

Now let's recount ourselves in terms of crisis dynamics
Depict the ends of state where history and the seas
Choose me since I see you there my dreamy fuck

Yr love for theory negates distinct periods involving
My words come out all wrong grossing much mulch
A lot of mulch not being elemental whereas history is

So many neo-liberal adjustments saying *yes we can*
Help condition yr profitability in exchange for the child
For whose realm of appearance I'm of the purest meat

And gas back then but now we're harder than gunboats

           — wiring each sentence fails to link us to real force.

●

for kari

No excuse for what appears explains
Spending hours on gas carriers poems
Being dumb share no reason no answer

For what's occurred keeps calling us
Here when seeming not to be ourselves
Recalling the violence yr signs go on

Appearing immediate lost and the grave
Exorbitance survives and gives and keeps
On giving this undoing proper kinship

Frames of fantasy an obscure gift we
Enter truth being the emptiness queerness
Names our sad selves ruins rubble fire feeds

This lack of product the only work to
Reason not the need to negate the world
Meaning meaning's pure excesses local

- izing sounds engendering riots in sense
Not sensing communion scandalizing death
In words with no future we seek portals

Holes and faults hew new relations quicken
Chasing that persistent and ongoing

– no!

COMMON
PLACE

A SQUARE, A CELL, A SENTENCE

this blank resource whose waste excels, a darker place where
bodies bend, ribs break in vaster banks, my blunting force,
just say whose organ, say whose bone, drafting futures, time
negated & not perceived as use, being raw, the stone, the
teeth, what strange glamour, hangs like a sun, this deciduous
mulch, the skin, the sky, the latch, the bone

in saying all this, let's say I've acquired a kind of money
function, or what stands in for that, I –

•

being of sound no prophecy feels, what the mind stands in for,
fallout from the coined relation, erosion of the working day
as a unit of measure, a calculable truth in whose place stands
my dutiful fuck, love's dirty interior, the fur-bound corn, my
sickly seed –

this eternity of stars repeating, whatever you make me
swallow I'll swallow, I say, hearing it again, imagining the
stone, his eyes like summer signs, suns of nature mask the
place of meanest meat, a blank concealed in every sentence

•

everything takes revenge on time, like debt, this surplus of
dead, my living décor, I swear on his balls, my very own
sucking stones, or coins, a ricochet of war and sex, the work of
human food, whatever skins intelligence, rude, like fate, such
rueful afterglow of what demise, mourning the passing of
system-wide reference, this allegory from which no soldier's
cock can be redeemed, deluge in which we find & fade

– such blips, sublime oblivions lurk, my whole interior being
one with their optics

•

my money scored to other scenes, this dreamy residue, an
aura of strangeness clings to his limb, a thing no longer here,
a plain where sheep-walks haunt the desire for landscape,
drowning dreams of nature as if the problem were one of
acreage, or ground rent, not being retinal, profit turns up in
my stool

– inside this scene, pure property of the deceased, for want
of luster, harvesting vacancies in which I'd have a share, if
only he would touch my mouth, plant his metal here

•

whose meat exposed for channel jamming, whatever it takes to conduct pure signal, the body clogging up no frame at all –

while hot lust fans, sheer weight the earth imagines, loins patch nerves the drill, these stones exchange for skin, the bone, the seed, the teeth, some pure emotion, like kerosene, or pomegranate, fiber of the stalk, the wreck, the phantom, I mean, my heart conceals an extremist core, being murderous, this puny mushroom, nothing refers anymore, all shares illiquid, no guarantee to resell

•

an exchange of coin, clean interior living, the fur, the wave, the wall behind which spread sublime fields, productive bodies get me hard inside the figures, yr deciduous mulch, meaning money, pure sound after periods of sonorous decay

all of them killed by abstractions nobody made –

inhabiting his thigh, singing it even, as if the destruction were too silent to know, wedded to limb turned to stump, this common place

•

a bone in my ass, where all future relation resides, if only
I could feel the structure of marketable risk, or even its idea,
the world entrenched inside his meat, worn lace, the latch

– to which I've attached my song, his fallen body, a ruse to
cure the nation, an obstacle wedged deep in old utopian zinc,
nothing empirical, the country wants to plug a dreamer's
lewd cognition, this feel for fucking without touching
anything at all

•

– along these interior roads, unmanned US drones, my vast
imagination, having led a mini-Tet offensive in the South,
whose shabby portion gleams and sewage glows, our one
true possibility, being false

beyond fascination, so excessively lit, as if there were light in
desolate cells, vision, being a security measure, like common
meat still longing for transport – just say the word *usufruct*
and levitate

·

his body, this omen to be waiting for, source of clarity, a
figure traced in stars, the bone, the lace, the tooth, the sky,
in whose shadow I go on believing in myself, succumbing
to old means, conditions under which I've prepared these
communications –

FALSE COMMUNIQUÉ

And so I sing this body on a table
For since the war I've read reports i
- magined events studied pro

- cedures assisting incarceration
W/ coroners who must know
Something and whose language

Rushes like unfettered streams on
- ly half-knowing the work I mean
Check out this wonder of a guy

A spectacle withdrawn & covered
With my latinate phrases issue
Displace so gorgeous a figure again

- st a ground of organs & viscera
For which the world moves its
Product making nothing this body

Linking it to that body my body
Severed from animal & plant over
Which production cycles steadily

Roll whose head the all-baffling
Brain eviscerates evacuates exa
- mines limbs jaundiced brown a

Cunning tendon nerve now strip
- ped so you still can't see things
But just imagine his dreamy eyes

Deadened plucked volition flakes
Inside pleural cavities mere sacs
Upon a table grey-white smooth

Mucosa distended stomach not
Flabby good-sized arms legs
Ureters & genitalia unremarkable

Interior what dura mater drapes
And mysteries haunt the clear
Yellow urine the pericardial bag

From which his prick might other
- wise rise normally with blood no
Longer running red runs to brown

Purple to tan as swelling jets pass
- ions patient swollen one would
Think not there since invisible

Condemned inside his fat the start
Of revolutions durable matter
Is thin delicate yielding countless

Embodiments baffling republics
Whose cranial nerves contest
My enjoyments will arrive

From the offspring of his offspring
Thru our bleakest time I come

– from him myself.

FALSE COMMUNIQUÉ

One civilian detainee was found
Unresponsive with a ligature
Or plastic band around my cock

A bottle ring pops pigeon death
In cell behavior health unit joint
Task force Guantanamo 2200 hours

When the ligature gets cut I come
Without remorse on the source
Of light his electric body being

Banished to mulch organic comp
- osition capital dividing luminous
Flux a rumor a burden of labor

Having fallen away from the tend
- ency of profit to rise and fall w/
The quality of radiance his cock

The way any man will use my hands
Like vitreous fluid his urine emits
So diffused a glow no needle-like

Beam thru pores of junk no evi
- dence of trauma resuscitation
Efforts begging immediate organ

- ization to turn blood back
To military cargo my skin
Now shares

                    – *with a tank.*

FALSE COMMUNIQUÉ

And as if to discredit all protest
- ant thought as ephemeral med
- ical treatment facility efforts fail

To revive [————] dead at 2300
Hours records reveal a ligature
Another absent cause whose

Effects themselves withdraw into
The fine textures of a detainee
- 's cauterized wounds whose emp

- tied bowels divide my poem's time
Between luminous flux & corporeal
Mass measured rate of increase where

- by the words surface expand & bloat
His body being a quandary or tension
Can reveal the nature of value being

Anti-social personality stressors
Confinement history of suicidal idea
- tion gestures & multiple failed

Attempts hunger involuntarily fed
And escorted in single point leg
Shackled w/ mask over mouth it

Keeps him from spitting biting
Swallowing the tongue liquidates
Whatever totality his dead body

Confirms the thing

— my pleasure negates.

His body like a slab of light bursts into this field of white. Now it's cooling down as my thoughts about him find their heat. The skin expels strange radiance, this blank wherein my writing hovers, it makes my tongue enlarge and my face break out, each organ yielding noisome fluid. Metal salts condense in the blood and amplify intensity. I need to believe this sentence follows the existence of something, a plosive hum or drone, an object in my head, whatever cuts on facial planes. Under grave prismatic glare, the tissue peels away, passing daily with my urine. The intestines shed internal slough, and we see it pass thru his rectum. Dead light emanates from such vague humors, concealing intravenous holes on his right arm and antecubital fossa. Such light is thrown upon my cornea, as the image stretches to inconceivable peripheries equal only to the surface area of rentable space where the appearance of military cargo becomes my own veil of particles. Subcutaneous fat cushions the emanation of even fainter waves, while the garbage that his organs make sublimes into profit, each marketable product sharing something of value with a tank. The arterial trachea, esophagus and tongue peel away in turn, as the body rejects each membranous surface, like a memory of home and the first bed I came in. What language overcomes the distance between this visionary space and the rational zone of the coroner's report to which his body's destined. His piss emits the same radiant glow, the way a pond in Thoreau's *Maine Woods* might glow, dividing luminous flux from the body's planar surface. For a moment I take his open skin for the source of my sentence. Serial sectioning of the brain reveals yet another scene of brilliance, as both stem and cerebellum emerge from the body in candescent gowns. On first sight, his light suggests a quality known to enhance the satisfaction of office employees, while allowing cannabis to grow strong and healthy, the same light needed for breeding poultry. His body's predicament, being just as rational, like the albuminous skin of an egg, erects its figure anterior to every gaze. Upon further sectioning, the cerebral hemisphere lets go a bulb of fire in a muted haze that dampens the atmosphere around this resting surface. A veneer of carbon waste, how it slumbers in my speech, the way his body dreams me here. The gurney no longer exists on solid ground, his body being an improper sexual object for which I ought to be sentenced. And so a meaning hangs over us, the structure of corporeal space, a crack between what we can perceive and what we can say. I make a little souvenir of hair and teeth glowing with residual heat, turning my pocket into a reliquary, my fantasy, his mausoleum. The body is thus secured inside a bean-sized hole, his limbs taxonomized, his face covered with luminous sores betraying a smooth pricing surface, a constellation of lesions through which the light moves in patterns that allow me to read the report. Plasma scrims through pores of junk, a beautiful pyrotechnic sun, a spasm of glass exploding from his skull. A needle-like beam protrudes through the epidermal tissue, and even wider bands transport the dura mater, each organ arrayed, bearing some concealed relation, now mechanically rendered visible. His penis, semi-erect, a feather of light now touching me gently. Cranial nerves spawn white arcs of joy, each of which perplexes, but whose quandary reveals true radiance, no evidence of trauma. A haptic rose, my dead giveaway. As always, the scandal is hushed in deep reserves of light. The secret of his sacred beam's no secret, but absolute exposure to rule, whose measures my darkness defies. Anyone who has looked directly at the source knows that this is only true.

Looking sadly at my cock, I begin rereading the autopsy report. 'A civilian detainee was found unresponsive in his cell with a ligature.' With no referent for what that word 'ligature' might denote, I imagine the metal clasp for securing a musical reed, like the dented one on my first clarinet, a thing with which I conducted my earliest experiments in masturbation, before the leather cord, the plastic cuff and clamp. I'm aroused by the suggestion of his body lying prone and feel myself getting hard, the way the structure of this sentence hardens around his figure, or the way a ligature disrupts the flow of oxygen to the dura mater, stimulating cell tissue due to a lack of endorphins, a deficit that has my pleasure centers craving. Upon being raised, his forehead reveals a cluster of dark lesions in which I can see my face breakout in the mirror. His gaze falls on my flaccid prick *evidence of injury* false promise of love moving thru thick undergrowth of ligament and sinew, suggesting a thicket of leaves and wood. As my hand searches for a thigh inside the pocket, a ligature becomes a thing of pleasure, like the plastic band of his institutional briefs, which I imagine removing with my teeth. Nothing requires more patience than the shadow of this thing pressing from above the bed. Hovering, a halo, the word 'ligature' assumes the importance of a punctum, contracting aura, at once instrument and vehicle of our transport. Were this elastic cord to be seen in some other light, it might be stretched along an empty horizon, coding as paradise, improving conditions of the general seizure. Like a musical slur, this surgical thread binds my letters. When lifted, his scrotum reveals my ligature's scar for photographs and documentation under enhanced illumination. This is how his punishment makes a memory of me, while the ligature links his body, at its most radically specific point, to the common good and its negation. And so, the individual case becomes one with universal interest, binding body & situation. For contrast, there's debridement, a surgical removal of dead tissue from a wound, where I can still recall fucking my soldier before pulling out in accord with a set of conventions, which, like grammar, govern the relations between subjects and objects within normal frames of reference, binding everything in advance to a deferred period, like my detainee's corpse, being the brightest moment in our repertoire of truth. His 'unremarkable genitalia' denoted in the report hint at the girth of a complementary hole, which reveals itself in the ligature's light as I kneel before him on the table. Serial incisions show no evidence of injury, as if his testicles had been shorn, served up in a deep ragout to compensate for hemorrhaged accounts, a cavity emptied of dura mater and replaced with my cum, which I collect in advance for very hygienic purposes, my poem, being still wired to the logic of future attacks. Peeled away, the skin reveals the extent of the ligature's reach, another absent cause, whose effects are themselves withdrawn into the fine textures of my detainee's cauterized sores. This truth no doubt follows the existence of something, a hill a cell a wood a limb, or the words for these things, which might themselves stand for nothing, a hole in militarized common sense, a body that repels every pronoun, open to the whole fucking assembly before which I tremble, naked and pathetic. I think you may be ready to enter the garden, he says. That's when I drive my tongue inside, like the general public anxious to see his balls snipped off with a pair of scissors, or his whole body disemboweled with a hot iron poker, or even more refined instruments issued by my corps of engineers. So I place the cord around his cock while looking sadly at my own, establishing equivalence between organs and garbage. He claims to be much older, without having achieved a single orgasm in his twelve years behind bars. Yr body, my devotional kink, what do I mean when I say 'I burn with love for you'? I'm still seeking a lyric structure that might allow me to ask this question, a sentence feeling for its own conditions but whose words continue to elude them, for example, 'On my knees, in the back of the cell, he holds my head to the rim of his latrine, just close enough for me to smell the crap he left there only an hour ago, and this fantasy turns me on to such a degree that I can feel a tiny bead of cum on the head of my dick, though I'm not even hard, as if whatever I'm breathing from that metal expanse might coincide with the limit of our episteme and the whole taxonomy of signs that make our life world visible at the expense of what can not appear here.' But I don't want this sentence to be an example of anything. Once his body is admitted and a relation felt, narrative returns like the repressed, which had been there all along, spilling over the structure of my sentence, awaiting its own improper content. Plastic flexi-cuffs around his hands, and a ligature said to be identical to the elastic band of his army-issued briefs, neutered on contact with my syntax, turning that part of him that has no name, the part to which my happiness clings, into the most fungible of things, his 'unremarkable genitalia'. Still, I can run my tongue along their edge, forcing arousal while reading this report where the wrongness of my object-choice feels unavoidable, like the limit of our knowledge where radical particularity is the hoax upon which the falseness of the universal hangs. Prone to auto-fellate, he achieves satisfaction without the assistance of this idea, but the ligature intensifies the pleasure of release as its tightening rigs the precarity of my own position, a body susceptible to change and unready to die. So I submit to what I can't master and spread my legs for his dreamy cock, remarkable for its perfect nest of shiny black hairs. There will always be someone who falls outside the general equality, being unimaginable from inside the frame. Take me on all fours, for example, his dick, being the most civic of fountains when he pisses on my face, a global rite, running like an alpine stream in Wordsworth's

Prelude. This makes the rupture visceral, like the purity of law whose victorious force polices our difference, now spreading with his penile girth, the heavy weight of a stallion's balls, diminished with his discharge, the total body being but an effect of its perceived effects. And so, I hollow out a cunt in his corpse to fuck a patient orifice *'opening to the other'*. This is how my love, in order to be love, is both enflamed and extinguished in the language of his 'unremarkable genitalia'. Addressing the flesh with serial sectioning, and still no evidence of trauma, I rub him down with alcohol and ignite the body, tightening the cord upon discharge, making further examination unnecessary.

TO BURN WITH LOVE (CODA)
for Sianne

There's nothing more politically transcendent
Said porn director & founder of Treasure
Island Studio than a cheap whore. It was

In an interview I found myself reading one
Afternoon in Dolores Park while thinking
About how to end this book which seems not

To want to end and he goes on by saying
That the body of the true whore is the flint
That makes the spark of revolution

Possible. Is this the spark I have in mind
When considering what it might mean to burn
With love for my detainee and I'm reminded

Of Baudelaire who in the Salon of 1859 writes
(And I can only paraphrase) it's not without
Some reason that I use the word *fantasy*

Which is all the more dangerous he says when
Unconstrained like the love inspired by a pro
- stitute as it falls into idiocy or degradation.

Fantasy throws light upon the obscurity
That obtains in things he goes on and if it does
- n't then the fantasy is horribly useless

Une inutilité horrible he calls it as if the promise
Of fantasy were strangely one to demystify
A mystified world wherein obscurity reigns or

To disenchant the enchanted while enchanting
That disenchantment in song. So if my song
Appears defiled perhaps it's only failed to shine

A light on its object to penetrate the appearance
Of things whose seeming transparency trans
- figures a useless horror whose own obscure

Abstraction is the use

        — to which it has been put.

WEAK LINKS

LEGEND

[————] ≠ place of future action, being choked inside a tube,
only the weakest

[————] ≠ surviving scenes of this undoing, a blank, or common
place, bodies wash up

[————] ≠ inside my interior, being a question of waste, remains,
and all that can't

[————] ≠ survive environment, now subtracting a false
irruption of birds, the buzz

[————] ≠ a null expanse, a local undoing, undermining refuse,
enhancing relations

[————] ≠ no remnant, equaling waste, disseminating methods,
eventuating seed

[————] ≠ futures, markets recall the body to itself, having been
this thing surviving

[————] ≠ identity's dreamy excess, in thrall to message,
achieving no place

[————] ≠ a hut, a border, a line, a tree, a method, a dead boy in
Gaza, or any residual

[————] ≠ subject, an unstoppable irruption, a tailbone poking
thru environment

[————] ≠ this skin, undoing what the war forces

Being so vehicular, roomy where my feet are
Tanks arrive inside, this way of picturing
Tall things go on lurching, limbs macerate
In public we reckon impossible tense, shame

On our own white floors, becoming impossible
Bodies extracted by the thousands, amassing
In a vault, margins, or a full-time occupation
These precedents bulk, my binding theme

•

Occurs, there being no such place as this at all
The imputation having been determined
So many erroneous self-images [————] skins
The hair and nails, our missing mortars, stumps

[————] pumping my disturbance with phonation
Days go by, open vowels, not generating much future
Sound [————] losses where all this will have happened

Any common place [————] strung out on being still
Produced disfigured gently now my ratcheted *dejecta*
[————] his leg becomes my fluted stump, my lip

His anal spur [————] missing tongues insert the word
Whose shock force grids resistant salvage, ours
Being squandered in advance, we molt in network

Fibers, having traced the place of future action
What can't be named in a field of roots, so come
Inside my fjord of mannered stools [————] watch

•

— the eyes peel back, so pasted to the blazing.

And in all these faces, the stills turn dark side up
Crushed to sand, a pink opaque erasing every sign

·

Of local need, the question of place remains beyond
Recognition [————] there being no foundation for the thing
To come, flooding tens of thousands, respectable merchants
All doing capital business when the awful news dissolves

Exchange, alluvial folds, our degraded interiors
        [————] shaping mutual alleviation, strains of want

                Diminishing, what you hear is the erosion
                        [————] of sound, this decay of tone

•

Come deeper now and kiss a little facial gum for steel
How yr system's beauty hovers in me, so shameful
Like rain clouds all the block-womb, antecedents
Boasting excess [————] this is fantastic, privation

In the language of plowmen, these extra folds
Skin and how we faked the needed hat disguise
Persona at the border, or some little article wedged
Between this failing organ [————] and that one

Opportunity shimmies slender faults to sanctum
I put my finger in his flap [————] still pulling back
For more, a so-called viscid white emulsion, or what
Ever it takes to make the ordnance take its target

Anything to ensure the proper bonding
Sickens in dehiscing blanks, a thickening
Trace achieves salvation [————] withering away
Gazing at events we still can't name

– and these have named us.

Shrill accords record [————] all these vibrations
Miming better reproductive techniques I have
Sown dark clouds above our bed the beautiful

Sounds of circuits memory and capital my treat
- ment of the subject won't save us from the total
Oblivion in becoming objective social fact

Collecting all the names and occupations
Yr sex will have been one of these [————]
Exhausted periods of glaciation coming from inside

The blanks I mirror his missing sounds all lip & throat
Compensate deficiency diminishing waste
[————] now admit our activist elements

– being nameless, we can sabotage the goods.

•

In place of something stands here, I, being serial
Dissent, attachments falling into salt-flats pumping
Up the so-called 'actual interconnection of all things'

Being a little blue today, green's the color, my terror
Alert all soft electrics, query cables crush the hold
Pursuant to what moves in waves, I'm harder still

Our gunboats spell a little haze above my stanza lags
There being way more beauty in that amputee than any
Cash could lend this place some real appeal

For all the off-shore crude, drilling broken facial steel
Limits no one credits for the mysteries of our turf

•

Now from the moss at lower elevations
[————] new monetary excitements come
Devouring the blanks exchanging signs
Trace nourishment, axing out our edifice

Lighten up yr load, recent avenues blocked
By the war or what stands in for [————] that
Being blocked by two bodies nobody saw
What's coming, being immaterial, he said

The crisis just reconstitutes what's known

— events now battered into bone.

•

I'm afraid [————] there's nothing more to say
From here we've been detained, as in a car park
And y're under [————] ground transmission
Spreading thru channels of our capillary

Mediations [————] there being nothing more
To apostrophize or summon, hails of nature
It seems so desperate, seeming still so hardened
No message lost in the overproduction of signal

Lost in my ear pressing up against yr hollow chest
Old nonsite delinking breath & word the scene
Of soldiers' bodies looted senses might report

•

the peculiar odor of our [————]

odium.

rain today, just need a little something to funnel down
the spine, it's this peculiar odor of dust, and ocher rising
from the softer growth, where some relation begins
to cohere, a place where no one lives anymore

I was thinking all this under duress & up against the wall
wondering how we ever got from then to now

having merely said this, having said this

·

FRAGMENTS OF
VULGAR THINGS

by Sam Ladkin

This is a simple book, an unfolding. It is also a vulgar book. *Placeholder* is careful, implacable, patient in its tenderness and sincere in its fantasies. I can't think of another book in which tenderness describes such a wealth of intimate obscenities quite so eloquently. It is a vulgar book in sharing its fantasies, written in our vernacular of love, violence, economics, and pornography. *Placeholder* understands how being explicit, which means unfolding, reveals what we might otherwise disguise (what Halpern calls the "haunting psychic backwash"), and hides beneath obscenities other painful truths. All this is treated with the tenderness longed for by an open wound.

Placeholder is not quite a selected poems, but rather one unfolding of the work Rob Halpern has been meticulously pursuing for over a decade. It is a book in which poems devoted to exposure have revealed themselves, also, as "so many strategies of evasion". Perhaps an assertion, often the most committed and unambivalent claim within a poem, begins to seem too assured, too much like it's concealing something feared. Or an idea expressed most vividly might turn out to have been another way of smothering disquiet, a way of evading the difficulties of one's life in each other's world. And so, at the risk of harming the work, and the person writing it, Halpern opens it up once more, disclosing what its light was hiding, the revelation of a new darkness.

It is a simple book, therefore, in eloquently unfolding its disquiet. Such revelations are essential to Halpern's practice. Consider 'House-Scrub', from the most recent collection *Common Place*, and how it speaks to 'Envoi', the opening poem of the previous *Music for Porn*. 'House-Scrub' describes how "any account of a logically coherent system must contain at least one radical instance that can't be contained by that account", and proposes the wound of a soldier as "just such an instance, a hole in sense, our common place, nonsite of suffering under current conditions, negative imprint of all my social relations." But inside the fantasy of the American military male that motivates *Music for Porn* we discover the repressed figure of the detainee; this is how the body of desire in one collection becomes the figure of incompletion for the next. Halpern writes, "There are so many things I've failed to tell you, things I'm still dying to share." This thing that cannot yet be said, the longed-for end to the fantasy, could be called love, although we cannot, yet, represent to ourselves the world worthy of that love.

In "Personism" Frank O'Hara famously placed the poem "squarely between the poet and the person, Lucky Pierre style", so that the poem might give and receive pleasure and be "correspondingly gratified". Rob Halpern's poetry, however, is on its knees. It is suppliant before bearers of power and before those who have none, in order to understand what power wants, and what power does. Halpern's poetry loves and longs for the sparkling wounds of bodies damaged in the West's fantasy of domination. Hence the title of this introduction is a dull-witted translation of Petrarch's suite of poems *Rerum vulgarium fragmenta*, now known as the *Rime Sparse* (scattered or disseminated verse), which disperses the singular body of its affections across its pages, offerings to the reader. Halpern, instead, writes love poetry for the bodies already broken and reified, strewn across the language we hold in common, and disavow, the laboring bodies of pornography, the wounded bodies of the soldier, and the tortured bodies of the detainee. These are bodies, as 'Whither Porn?' describes them, mediated by "regimes of representation *property and selfhood*", whether they are the "bodies I love or the countless others withdrawn in scenes of conflict and catastrophe and to which my body is joined thru flows of arms and money".

Placeholder marks a particularly good moment to look back on Halpern's devastating achievement. With the publication of *Common Place* (Ugly Duckling 2015) we can now return through the whole series, past *Music for Porn* (Nightboat 2012), *Imaginary Politics* (Tap Root

Editions 2008), *Weak Link* (Slack Buddha 2007), *Disaster Suites* (Palm Press 2009), all the way to *Rumored Place* (Krupskaya 2004). That book, "so unresolved and in flight from itself", is where we first meet the black bar [————] for which "placeholder" is a stub.

The collection you hold retains a sense of the logic of the original order of publication, whilst the first section has been assembled from various published and unpublished material to give an introduction to the work as a whole. What follows are three set pieces; the earliest from *Rumored Place*, before pieces from *Music for Porn*, and the most recent material from *Common Place*. Two discordant notes from *Disaster Suites* interrupt this sequence. You can see the book unfold from and return to its earliest concerns. Halpern looks to liberate that which subsists in rumor (referencing Robert Duncan's 'This Place Rumord to Have Been Sodom') in order to legislate for the unacknowledged commons. *Music for Porn* is therefore at the heart of *Placeholder*. Where lyric love poetry traditionally carries its own music, *Music for Porn* replays lyric's music in our age of disenchantment. The phrase "music for porn" is Halpern's proposed definition of lyric in the age of technological reproducibility in which we find that the alienation of our most intimate affections retains some remainder of utopian happiness. The final section is collated from *Weak Link*, not so much a conclusion to the collection as a final weakening. Rather than a modest assertion of doubt in the achievements of this poetry, the end expresses a desire to loosen the ties that bind us: "Of local need, the question of place remains beyond / Recognition". We must leave room in the description of where we are now – our place – for a utopia that cannot yet be represented. The future is unrecognizable, and cannot be an image from our memories alone (that is, recognized) but must be radically rethought; Halpern wants us to know how to share that impasse, to hold dissent in common. The writing here will welcome you, and discuss with you its hopes, and the intractability of its failings, failings in which we all abide.

The book in your hands has been redacted. It does what it can to make explicit what has been covered up. The black bar of a redaction, a blanking out, is that which occludes the proper name of a detainee on an autopsy report from Guantanamo, an occultation in language akin to the prohibition on images of the coffins, and their corpses, returning from war to the US. When we use the term redaction we tend to imagine documents blackened by authority, but to redact has meant to bring together, to gather in a place, to compile multiple sources into a single document. *Placeholder* holds the place of the earlier collections. Its black bar [————] is an aporia, meaning 'without passage', that which we cannot easily overcome, a sign marking an absence as we wait, impatiently, as "patients of history", for some alternative to the contradictions of our times. The aporia enforces doubt, since the brutal certainty of the body in pain cannot be shared, and yet must be held in common. Our contradictions are outsourced in the body "where incommensurables collide." The black bar is an elision rather than a sign, *"placeholder for all we can't perceive haunting all we can* like the mark of something withdrawn from sense." The black bar offers some space of hope for a future that cannot yet be resembled. The black bar [————] is a mark of redaction, a mark occluding a sign, a cover-up in legalese for the atrocities being placed silently on the record, a redaction of the pain of no future. Aporia, impasse between transparency and obscurity, bodies we cannot see obscured by the spectacularization of those we can.

Sam Ladkin
Brighton, 2015

ACKNOWLEDGMENTS

The poems included in this volume are drawn from across a long project that has occupied my writing since the mid 2000s and for which I've adopted the sign [————] to stand in lieu of a proper title. Under the internecine conditions of never ending enclosures – by military & finance, nation & police – I imagine this sign as a place-holder for a common world, the world we radically long for but whose advent is blocked by those conditions, the world whose beauty we know in dreams and whose plenty we can taste already, the world whose realization will make these poems irrelevant.

Most of the work collected here has been lifted from the following books: *Rumored Place* (Krupskaya 2004); *Disaster Suites* (Palm Press 2007); *Music for Porn* (Nightboat Books 2012); and, *Common Place* (Ugly Duckling Presse 2015), as well as two chapbooks, *Weak Link* (Slack Buddha Press 2007) and *Imaginary Politics* (Tap Root Editions, 2008). The poem "Snow Sonnet" appears in *Snow Sensitive Skin*, a book length poem written in collaboration with Taylor Brady (Atticus/Finch 2007, reissued in an expanded edition by Displaced Press in 2011). A debt of gratitude is due to all the publishers and collaborators. "Prelude to Commodious" (for Peter Linebaugh), "This Cell in My Head Is Made of Wax" (for Thom Donovan), and "An Essay on the Siege" appear here in book form for the first time.

While many of the assembled poems are grouped under the aegis of this or that book, the collection does not obey any strict chronolog-ical order, nor is it meant to be a mere sampling. Rather, [————] aims for its own integrity as a sound figure, while preserving fidelity to a larger canvas.